## SMALL BUSINESS TOOLKIT

# *Sales for the*
# *Self-Employed*

SMALL BUSINESS TOOLKIT

# Sales for the Self-Employed

## MARTIN EDIC

PRIMA PUBLISHING

© 1997 by Martin Edic

PRIMA PUBLISHING and colophon are trademarks of Prima Communications, Inc.

**Library of Congress Cataloging-in-Publication Data**

Edic, Martin.
    Small business toolkit : sales for the self-employed/Martin Edic.
        p.  cm.
    Includes index.
    ISBN 0-7615-0593-8
    1. Selling.  2. Self-employed.  3. Small business  I. Title.
HF5438.25.E34      1997
658.8—dc21                                                      96-50056
                                                                   CIP

97 98 99 00 01 HH 10 9 8 7 6 5 4 3 2 1

Printed in the United States of America

**How to Order**

Single copies may be ordered from Prima Publishing, P.O. Box 1260BK, Rocklin, CA 95677; telephone (916) 632-4400. Quantity discounts are also available. On your letterhead, include information concerning the intended use of the books and the number of books you wish to purchase.

Visit us online at http://www.primapublishing.com

# CONTENTS

Acknowledgments xi

Introduction: Communicating and Solving Problems xiii


**Section One:**
**PROSPECTING 1**

**Chapter 1: The Sales Challenge 3**
Selling Is Communicating 5
The Process—Five Basic Steps 7

**Chapter 2: A Little Geology 13**
Targeting 14
Products Are Solutions 20

**Chapter 3: Prospecting Tools 27**
The Prospecting Process 28
The Toolkit 30

**Chapter 4: First Contact 45**
Your Personal Investment 47
Their Personal Investment 47
Friendly Aliens 52
Professional Communicator 55

**Chapter 5: The Appointment 57**
A Designated Time Slot 58
Your Undivided Attention 59
Preparation 59

Long-Distance Selling   61
Proposals, Estimates, and Quotes   62
Ending the Meeting   63
Review and Follow-Up   63
Saying No   64

**Chapter 6: Training Yourself   67**
Subconscious Selling   68
Conscious Selling   69
Learning   71
Visual, Auditory, Kinetic   71
The Outside Perspective   73
Rehearsal   75
Persistence   77

**Chapter 7: Fear and Rejection   79**
Negative and Positive   81
Goals   84
Rejection   84

**Chapter 8: Your Sales Plan   87**
Time   87
Leverage   88
Writing Your Sales Plan   89

**Section Two:**
**SELLING AS A PROCESS   97**

**Chapter 9: The Communications Process   99**
Process and Content   101
Success Without Selling   102
Listening   104

**Chapter 10: The Problem-Solving Model  107**

Problems  108

The Sizzle and the Steak  109

Convincing People to Buy  110

Solutions  111

Products As Solutions  113

**Chapter 11: Needs and Desires  115**

Getting Beyond Needs  116

Discovery  119

**Chapter 12: Presentation
          Research and Materials  123**

Research  124

Presentation Materials  128

**Chapter 13: Meet and Greet  141**

First Impressions  144

AIDA  145

Visual Impressions  146

Kinetic Impressions  147

Tone of Voice  148

**Chapter 14: Qualifying  153**

Qualified Buyers  154

Identifying the Core Problem  159

Listening Skills  169

Attention  169

## Chapter 15: Presenting    173

Presentation Step One: Your Background    174

Presentation Step Two: Your Capabilities    176

Presentation Step Three:
   Your Solution and Your Price    177

Presentation Step Four: Shut Up    178

Quotes and Estimates    179

Presenting Style    180

Objections    182

## Chapter 16: Trial Close    185

Conditional Closing    187

Spend Time to Save Time    188

## Chapter 17: The Close    191

Agree to Buy    192

Agree on the Value    193

Good-Faith Deposit    195

Put It in Writing    195

Agree on a Time Frame    196

Deliver the Goods    196

Closers Wanted    197

## Chapter 18: Delivery    199

Negative News Travels Fast    201

Our Town    201

Completed Work    202

Demonstration    206

Wrapping It Up    207

## Section Three:
## THE SALES LIFE   209

## Chapter 19: Follow Up Forever   211

Follow-Up Planning   212
Future Sales   213
Referrals   216
Thank You   218
Time and Past Customers   219

## Chapter 20: Proposal Selling   221

RFPs   222
Project Proposals   225
Timing   226
Proposal Follow-Up   226
Promises, Promises   227
Speculative Proposal Selling   228
Change-of-Life Proposals   231

## Chapter 21: Motivation   233

From Beginning to End   234
Developing Your Own Motivational Process   235

## Chapter 22: Incentives   245

Enticing Rewards   246
Using Incentives to Motivate Yourself   250
Incentives to Buy   252
Bird-Dog Programs   254

## Chapter 23: Negotiation   257

Information and Time   259
Making an Offer   260

Everything Is Negotiable   261
Risk Management   262

**Chapter 24: Invisible Selling   265**
Rapport   266

**Chapter 25: Improving Your Product   277**
Customizing Your Products   279
Developing New Products   283

**Chapter 26: Sales Tools   289**
Time Management   289
Volunteer Work   291
Public Speaking   292
Customer Database   292
Exercise and Nutrition   294
An Open Mind   294
Fast Response   295
Shop Talk   296
Sales Tools for Tomorrow   296

**Resources:   301**
Books   301
Magazines and Periodicals   304
Miscellaneous   305

Index   307

# ACKNOWLEDGMENTS

Selling is an activity you learn from doing and observing. The experience of other sales professionals I've worked with has made my understanding of the process much clearer. Thanks to Arnie Sprague, Scott Pundt, Don Mook, Dan Deutsch, Paul Dodd, Peggi Fournier, and the many other people I've worked with over the years who shared both their knowledge and experience with the art of selling. And lest I forget, to my customers who are, as the saying goes, always right.

# INTRODUCTION

## COMMUNICATING
## AND SOLVING PROBLEMS

Every business, large and small, depends on a few vital skills for both survival and success. Perhaps most important are the ability to clearly communicate with your customers and the ability to provide solutions for the problems they face. For the self-employed small business owner, these skills become doubly important because the responsibility for learning and using them falls directly on you. You are the business.

Sales is the business activity where these two vital skills are most important. To successfully sell your products or services, you must find prospective customers, communicate with them to discover their needs or problems, and then show them how you can provide a solution for those problems.

You'll notice that I don't talk about convincing customers, talking them into things, making them buy, or any other strong-arm techniques. Instead, the vital words remain *communicate, solve problems,* and *show.* There is a good reason for this approach. Many of us have an aversion to selling, viewing it as a necessary evil—or at best, an unfortunate task. Much of this distaste comes from a misunderstanding of what selling is. Selling is not talking people into things they don't want, selling is offering them solutions to problems they face and making it easy for them to acquire these solutions.

*Sales for the Self-Employed* is for the business owner who is not a sales professional, although I believe readers with considerable sales experience will still find it interesting. It teaches selling as a step-by-step process and a skill that you can learn and enhance through regular practice. Of course, as a self-employed person, you have many things to do besides selling. For this reason I've stressed an approach to sales that seeks to streamline the process wherever possible. Sales doesn't need to take much out of your day if you focus on the best prospective customers before you start to sell and make sure you prepare yourself as completely as possible before you say a word.

Beyond the potential for increased business and profits that comes from successful selling, there is another benefit. Selling is a fascinating thing to do. You meet and interact with all kinds of people. You learn about their businesses and lives and you often have the opportunity to enhance those lives. You also learn a great deal about what you do and why you're doing it. Self-employment is rarely a decision made strictly for financial benefit. It is a lifestyle choice based on a desire to control your own destiny. Every aspect of it should be equally interesting because you are doing it for yourself.

Selling your own work means you should have no qualms about what you're selling. You can be totally enthusiastic and your customers will believe you. In this sense, a self-employed person making a sales presentation has an advantage over our wage-earner friends: We do what we do because we want to—and that includes selling.

Read the book through, make notes—mental or in black and white—and think about your previous sales experience as a comparison. I think much of what you'll find here is simple common sense about a process we've all practiced since early childhood: communicating and solving problems.

## A NOTE ABOUT TERMS

In this book, I always use the word *customer* rather than client or any other descriptive word. While—like many professionals—you may not like to think of yourself as dealing with anything so pedestrian as an ordinary customer, your clients, guests, and partners (choose your terminology) are all customers. You sell something, they buy. For the sake of simplicity, let's agree that when I say customer, I mean all the rest too.

Another area of confusion is the distinction between products and services. Most people think of products as something manufactured in multiples and services as unique actions taken for someone. From a marketing and sales perspective, they are all products. If you consult for a living, your product is your experience and expertise—as it is with almost every service business. You can add to your product mix by learning new skills just as store owners add to theirs by carrying new lines. Again, for simplicity's sake, I just call everything we sell products.

SMALL BUSINESS TOOLKIT

# Sales for the Self-Employed

# SECTION ONE

# PROSPECTING

# CHAPTER 1

# THE SALES CHALLENGE

When you choose self-employment, you to a certain degree choose a solitary existence. In other words, when it comes to many aspects of running your business, you're on your own. You may not have support staff to take care of accounting, buying supplies, answering phones, and all the other little tasks that make up much of the daily grind of business ownership. You are the cook, bottle-washer, captain, and deckhand on your ship. This single-handed existence is part of the intriguing challenge that makes many of us feel that self-employment is the only employment we want.

There is another aspect to the challenge of being in business on your own. No one is going to bring customers to you, ready, willing, and able to buy your products or services. You may start out with a few select customers from previous work relationships, plus some relatives or friends. These "complimentary" customers can help you get started, but few businesses can survive on the needs of such a limited group. Eventually, you must go out into the world and find and convince new, unknown people to buy from you. This is the sales challenge—and those who do not embrace it willingly are likely to fail.

All too often, the self-employed business person views selling as a necessary evil. A lot of us would like to work away at our skills, never taking the plunge into the world of prospecting, negotiating, educating, and problem solving that is the world of sales. We have been conditioned from early on to mistrust anyone who is trying to convince us to buy, even when we have a strong need for the product they're selling. There is a saying in the sales world that people love to buy but hate to be sold. But is it true?

Mention the word *sales* and the first thing that probably comes to mind is an unfortunate experience with a car salesperson or a pushy clerk in an appliance store. Even if we have a great experience buying a car, we tend to view it as a battle in which we have somehow triumphed over the forces of greed and evil. Yet every day, millions of people happily buy billions of dollars worth of every imaginable commodity, and in almost every case they have dealt with a sales professional. It is a paradox.

The reality is that sales and selling is the lubricant of a market economy, keeping the flow of goods moving, creating every job, and making every successful business profitable. There are no exceptions. Without a sales effort, conscious or unconscious, you will not succeed in your business. In fact, small business studies and success profiles show that effective sales skills are the number one requirement for success in any small business. Sales ability ranks above money, commitment, innovation, and intelligence. No amount of these talents can get you market share without some selling—and without market share you have no cash flow. Selling is survival.

## SELLING IS COMMUNICATING

Fortunately, selling is much more than a survival technique. It is a whole panorama of interesting and challenging skills, experiences, and learning opportunities. It's human interaction, education, and motivation. Ultimately, the ability to sell is the ability to communicate effectively with a wide range of diverse people.

Is it a talent? We often hear about "natural born salespeople" who somehow have an edge over the rest of us. We repeatedly convince ourselves that we have no such natural ability until the words resonate in our heads whenever we consider selling. I don't believe in natural sales ability or the lack thereof. What I do know is that some people have persistence and motivation and work constantly on their skills and that these people make great salespeople. They also make great bakers, consultants, graphic designers, athletes, and politicians. They tend to be attracted to working on their own and succeeding or failing on their own merits. Sound familiar? It's the same profile that leads to choosing self-employment as a way of life.

## You're a Natural

We all have good sales skills when it comes to getting what we want, especially when we're young. Children regularly gather information about a desired toy or event and batter their parents relentlessly with that information. They use sales techniques that would make the slimiest used car dealer back off—including blackmail, intimidation, acting out, hunger strikes, declarations of war, and withholding of love to achieve their desires. When they win, it is usually because they have eventually discovered the secret to all successful sales: solving a problem. The fact that they may have created the problem in the first place doesn't mean that it is any less dire by the time their parents cave in.

## Problems and Solutions

While you could employ the drastic sales techniques you used as a child in your business, I doubt they would work as well for you now. We're adults and we don't accept such behavior from our peers. Even if we did buy, we would never return and would undoubtedly steer others away from such a nasty individual. Because the success of most self-employed people depends on repeat business and referrals, the unrepentant childlike seller would soon be out of business.

Fortunately, there is an important lesson embedded in these childhood experiences. The way to get someone interested in your work is to offer a solution to a pressing problem they have. You don't need to be a quivering bundle of raging charisma to do this. You simply need to make a connection, learn about the problem, present a valuable solution, and ask for the business. This is the basic process of selling, underlying every transaction between humans: meeting, gathering information, identifying problems, offering solutions, and agreeing to terms. This book attempts to help self-employed people like yourself understand sales as a process and to learn that process so you can apply it your individual business.

## THE PROCESS—FIVE BASIC STEPS

The core of this book is a simple, step-by-step process that can be applied to any kind of sales. In some cases, you may go through the entire process in a few moments; in others, it may take as long as a year or more—but you'll find that every successful transaction involves all of these steps. The steps all come after research to discover prospects and product knowledge that helps you offer solutions. Section One of *Sales for the Self-Employed* covers this preliminary research. And after the sale, there are several vital steps that can lead to repeat business, referrals, and the development of better selling skills. You'll find these in the third section of the book. The actual sales process is in the middle. For now, though, let's go over it quickly so you'll have an idea how it works as you read and learn.

All sales occur as part of a five-step process. Learn it and you can learn to sell. Ignore it and your sales experience will be a confusing mishmash. I started out selling in a retail store with absolutely no training. We walked up to customers and asked them if we could help them. They almost always said they were looking and moved on. After that I sold real estate. My broker ran a small office and believed that you learned on the job. He gave us a personal form of sales training that chiefly consisted of watching him and listening to his anecdotes about how customers behaved. His favorite line was "buyers are liars," something he often repeated. Not only was this maxim untrue, it reinforced a negative view of our entire customer base before we even met them!

In spite of spotty training, I did fairly well selling houses, having good months and bad and eking out a living. I knew there must be a better way but remained ignorant of how to sell. There were training classes available, but my broker didn't think they helped. Finally I drifted on to a related job that didn't involve selling.

Sales had made a positive impression on me, though. I missed the feeling you get from matching customers with purchases that enhance their lives. And I missed the commission pay structure that rewards your efforts. On a whim, I went out and applied to a major local car dealer for a sales position and was hired. The first thing I did upon starting work was get ushered into the weekly Monday morning sales meeting. And there something very interesting happened.

I sat down with about ten other salespeople, and the sales manager got up and went over to a blackboard and asked the group who could name the five steps to successful selling. Everybody but me raised their hands and as they reeled off their answers, he wrote them down on the board. They were:

1. Meet and Greet
2. Qualify
3. Present
4. Trial Close
5. Close

I looked at the first with a mystified gaze. Meet and greet? This sounded pretty corny. The others meant little—except for closing. I thought I knew what that was, and I knew it was hard. By the time I quit selling cars and went to work for myself a year later, however, I had each step down cold. If I was having trouble with a customer, I'd go to that same sales manager and he would go over the list, making sure I'd covered each step. If I'd skipped one, he would send me back to do it. The steps worked and they made most of us into salespeople.

## Meet and Greet

The first step is a simple one. All you have to do is introduce yourself and make a great first impression, and things will go swimmingly. But what is a great first impression? It's harder than it looks. And there is seldom a second chance. Learning to meet and greet potential buyers is a vital skill.

## Qualify

You qualify a customer by asking questions and listening. The goal is to discover two basic things: What they want and whether they are capable of making a buying decision. Neither is a cut-and-dried proposition. Customers may not consciously know what they want. You must identify the problems they want to solve by buying your product or service. All of the problems. And you must make sure you're dealing with the right person. The right person is the one who makes the decisions and signs the checks. If you give your sales presentation to the wrong person, you're going to be going through it all over again when and if you find the decision maker.

## Present

Showtime. But it's not a performance. You may use a canned presentation, and with certain products it may work. Most of the time, your presentation will start out with an overview of the basic features of your product and then address the benefits. What are benefits? The features that solve those problems you uncovered in your qualifying step. Miss any and you may not succeed.

## Trial Close

How do you know if you missed anything? You use a trial close. A close means closing the deal by asking the customer to buy. A trial close tests the waters. You might say: If I can provide X feature and Y feature the way you need them, will you buy? If they say yes, you go to the close. If they say no, you go back to step two and find the unresolved problem.

## Closing

We just said that closing was asking someone to buy. Please think carefully about that. You must ask someone to take action, usually involving money, in order to complete the sale. Amazingly enough, this is all there is to the mysterious process of closing, provided you did all the other steps completely. In fact, if you really did all those steps, you don't need to close! It happens all by itself. You too can be a closer.

■ ■ ■

So now you know all my secrets. You can write down the five steps on a 3 × 5 card and keep it in your pocket.

When you're in a sales situation, just check them off as you do them and you'll do fine.

The End.

Wait a minute. It couldn't be that simple, could it? The answer is it can and it's not. The process is simple, deceptively so. Learning to use it effectively is a lifelong process, one that will change the nature of your life as a self-employed person. You'll know more about what you do, why you do it, and why anyone would want to pay you for it. You'll learn a lot about how people communicate since you must become a consummate communicator to get through the process successfully. And you must become a great listener, the kind that strangers tell their innermost secrets to. It doesn't hurt to be a little bit like a counselor, a coach, a consultant, and an artist, either. Great selling involves more than a little of each.

Like the five-step process itself, this book has to start at the beginning. And the sales process doesn't begin until you find a customer. Not just any customer, a motivated, prosperous, willing customer who really needs your product. Of course no one is a customer until he or she has made a purchase. Until then, they're prospects. And to find prospects you must go prospecting.

# CHAPTER 2

# A LITTLE GEOLOGY

Before anyone becomes a customer, he or she is a prospective customer—a *prospect,* in sales lingo. Depending on what it is that you sell, your prospects can range from almost anyone on the planet to a very few select individuals who have a specific need for your products. Selling something like food that everyone needs is very different from selling something very specialized like computer network consulting. If you own a grocery store, your prospects are so universal that you really don't need to do any prospecting to find the ideal customer. Anyone on the street is a likely prospect.

However, as a self-employed person you almost certainly have a much narrower potential market—it is in the nature of being self-employed to be a specialist. You must go prospecting to find those specific people who have a demonstrated need for your products and the ability to pay for them. Before you do any selling, you need customers—and the more targeted you are in seeking those customers, the easier it will be to sell to them.

## TARGETING

Target markets are groups of people who share a similar set of demographics—similar lifestyles, interests, income and education levels, backgrounds, and so on. When you're selling a very specific set of solutions (your product) you need to target your efforts at groups of people whose demographic profiles fit your market. Before this gets too confusing, let's look at it another way.

The word *prospecting* originally meant searching for valuable minerals or resources like gold or oil. Prospectors used everything from rumor to practical experience to find likely spots before they started digging. Now geologists use their knowledge of geological science to identify areas likely to produce riches. They look at local geology, rock formations and makeup, and overall global geology including things like plate tectonics that tell them where the mineralogical action is. Only after comparing hundreds of potential sites and doing exhaustive research will they recommend the expense and massive effort of digging a mine. They use their preliminary research to minimize risk and maximize return.

The prospecting for likely customers that you do will have the same result. If you picked ten people at random from a crowd and gave them your sales pitch, you would be lucky to sell to even one of them, no matter what you were selling. If you put together a demographic description of people likely to need your product and targeted a group of ten people with both a proven need and a known ability to pay, your closing ratio (or sales success rate) would be much higher, perhaps even 100 percent!

The importance of this aspect of the sales process cannot be underestimated. If you do an excellent job of prospecting to find an ideal customer group for your business, the sales process will become immensely easier and far less mysterious. You will spend less time explaining, little time cajoling, and no time talking people into anything because they will already have a defined need for your products and a demonstrated desire to buy. If you are lucky, you'll become what many so-called professional salespeople often deride: An order taker.

## Order Takers

In the sales profession, *order takers* are salespeople who sit and take orders from anyone who walks in or calls needing their products. They don't pitch, close, or hammer their customers; they simply take orders. Salespeople who must fight for every order and go out and constantly drum up new business put down order takers as unimaginative and unskilled clerical types. I see it a little differently.

As a self-employed person, you are not just a professional salesperson, you are a business owner. Your interest is in generating work, income, and profits, not just sales. For many of us, being order takers would be an almost ideal situation. We'd sit in our offices or shops, and customers would come to us ready and willing to buy on the spot. Sounds pretty good, doesn't it?

The degree to which you are a salesperson instead of an order taker is determined by marketing and the type of business you're in. Marketing is everything you do to bring customers to you prior to the sales process and everything you do afterward to ensure their loyalty and generate future business. Sales is part of the marketing process, the vital part where you turn prospects into customers. In this chapter and the ones that follow in the first section of *Sales for the Self-Employed,* we're going to look at the research and marketing you must do to put you in contact with the best prospective customers for your business. You're going to learn your own science of sales geology and how to find the signs and formations that point you to the gold.

## Customer Profiling

I'm going to assume you already know something about your customers, even if you're just starting out. That knowledge may not be accurate (or even useful), but it will serve to get us started creating a profile of a typical customer for your products. Start by listing any common attributes your current customers share. Some to consider include:

- Age.
- Income range.
- Location.
- Education (including number of years and major interest).
- Job description.
- Interest group membership (including associations, industry or academic groups, hobbyist groups, and so on).
- Sex, religious background, ethnic background, race, and so on. Note: You need this kind of information to help you find and sell to your prospects, not as exclusionary criteria. The more you know, the better equipped you are to serve their needs.

As you consider each likely or proven customer, make notes of any attributes or interests that are common to the majority. These are pointers that can lead you to like-minded people who may share a need for your products. They also help you to create profiles of highly profitable customers so that you can go out into the marketplace and focus your sales efforts on similar prospects.

## Ten Prospects for Success

The value of taking the time to profile good customers and target similar groups is particularly high for self-employed people because we often don't need large numbers of customers to prosper. In fact, this is the great advantage we have over large companies with large overhead who must sell great quantities to earn enough profit. The average self-employed person will probably do very well adding as few as one to ten new customers each year, particularly if those customers are exceptional. But what is an exceptional customer?

Let's look at John, who runs a landscaping company specializing in designing, building, and maintaining small but beautiful garden areas for urban dwellers and businesses. John's edge is the fact that he offers one-stop shopping: He plans, builds, and maintains, making it easy for his customers to have the garden they want without dealing with numerous contractors. The downside of his business is that his hands-on approach limits him to doing a relatively small number of gardens.

John's customers are highly educated urban home-owners who are in a high income bracket and often hold executive positions or own their own businesses. They have limited time but a lot of disposable income. Once they contract with John, they typically stay customers until they move or retire. He services about 25 homes and businesses and has a turnover of about 20 percent a year, requiring that he add 5 customers annually to maintain his current sales level. If he wants to grow, he should be adding around 10 per year.

The challenge for John is to find the 10 exceptional customers who will not only stay with him for years but will also make regular referrals. He already knows what type of people they will be and where he is likely to find them in his city. He can target his marketing efforts directly at these demographically distinct individuals. His ads, brochures, and networking will focus exclusively on the best prospects, and the responses they generate will be prequalified before he starts the sales process.

In addition to making the sales process much easier, targeting also helps generate referrals, references, and networking opportunities. A landscaper like John will be in regular contact with his customers, and their friends will see the results of his labors. This will generate referrals—and strong referrals often do not require any selling other than price and schedule negotiations. He will also get various networking opportunities, including invitations to social occasions and community get-togethers that his customers attend. By sharing this part of their lifestyle, he becomes an even more likely resource for them to refer others to.

## Relationship Selling

John's selling style is based on developing valuable and mutually beneficial customer relationships that generate rewards for both parties. The exceptional customers you should be seeking will expect something of value from their relationship with you. The values most prized in a business relationship are trust, quality, time, and money. Offer these to the right group of prospects, and your selling will become much easier.

Prospecting for exceptional customers and preparing your products so that they completely fulfill those customers' needs can take much of the mystery out of sales. Target the right customer groups, send the message they want to hear, and provide the stellar service they expect—and your sales will close themselves. Skip these steps and you'll spend a lot more time selling and have a much lower ratio of success to failure.

Knowing your prospective customers' lifestyles and reaching out to them are only part of the whole prospecting process. You must also tailor your products to fit their needs and desires. The more perfect the fit between product and customer, the easier the sale.

## PRODUCTS ARE SOLUTIONS

The entire sales process involves solving problems for your customers. Those solutions are not always the obvious ones inherent in your product. A financial planner may see the real benefit of her work as a significant increase in future income for clients. The clients, however, may see it very differently—as a way to reduce stress and anxiety about not preparing properly for the future. The stress may be related to fear or ignorance that keeps them from taking action to help themselves. The financial planner solves that problem by coming in and relieving that stress by offering a way to take the first steps. The planner thinks she's selling future security, but the reality is that she is selling stress relief right now. By tailoring her product presentation to address these immediate fears in addition to the long-term benefits, she'll remind her clients of the relief they need now.

Everything you offer to any prospective client is a product—no matter if it consists of things, services, advice, psychological benefits, increased income, or other and less tangible results. Before you go out to sell, you must consider your products from every angle—with particular focus on how they look from the customer's viewpoint. We tend to know our own products from a features point of view, whereas our customers think of them in terms of what benefit they will derive from them. This features-benefits pairing is a classic advertising technique that you should learn and use when developing and promoting new products and services.

## Features and Benefits

Analyzing what you do from a features-benefits point of view may be an enlightening experience—the things you consider powerful features may not resonate with your customers, while things that you haven't considered can be vital selling points. A powerful sports car may have a 200-horsepower engine, leather seating, power windows, and so on, all of which are features. The benefits of those features are a different story. They tend to be much more visceral and emotional—a return to youth, a feeling of personal power, a statement of status and success, things like that. While you might cover the technical features of your product in your ads and sales presentation, you must address these emotional benefits as you cover each technical item. For instance, you'd stress the feel of the cool leather, the powerful acceleration and throaty roar of the engine, and the exclusivity of owning such a rarefied beast.

There is a simple exercise you can do to learn more about how a customer might view your products; it's called a *features-benefits comparison*. Advertising copywriters often do this exercise before they sit down to write compelling ad copy about a new product. It helps them identify the "hot button" benefits of that product that will grab attention and create immediate interest in owning it.

Start with a blank sheet of paper for each product or service you offer. Divide it into two vertical columns and title the left-hand one Features and the right-hand one Benefits. On the Features side, list all of the technical features of your business. Specifications, specialized experience and skills, tools you have, locations, previous client names, and any other things you think are important about what you offer. On the Benefits side, next to each feature, write down the actual benefits to the customer of that feature. Benefits include saving or making money, saving time, relieving stress, enhancing self-esteem or business success, fixing emergencies or broken items, and so on. There must be a clear benefit for you to write down. If a feature has no corresponding benefit, put a line through it—it has no place in your sales presentation or marketing.

A good example of a feature that may have no real benefit is a fancy office. If you have a nice office in a prestigious location but seldom have clients in that office for meetings, it is not a benefit. It may make you enjoy your work more, which benefits you—but it is not a selling point. In some businesses, the appearance of success is very important because it conveys a sense of security and the feeling that the customer may share in your success, both of which are compelling benefits. In others, the appearance of excessive prosperity may turn off customers. I remember one very successful local real estate agent who saw her sales of middle-class homes slide after she purchased an expensive German car. Her clients picked up the idea that she was a little too concerned with getting their money. When she switched back to a minivan similar to the ones her typical clients drove, she started selling again.

Once you start to learn the benefits of your products, you'll have a clearer idea of how they appeal to your customers and you'll spot areas where you need to strengthen them. Look at all the things you are selling and at the demographic profiles of your best customers and change the things that don't directly benefit those customers. You may not have to eliminate anything; you're more likely to add benefits or only sell the features that you know will appeal to a specific customer. When we look at the qualifying process in Section Two, we'll see how to identify these compelling features.

### Never Leave a Feature Hanging

From now on, there is rule you must follow until it becomes a habit: Whenever you mention a feature of what you do, you must immediately describe the benefit to your customers of that feature. Never leave a feature hanging. If I tell a prospect that my recording studio has a Web page on the Internet, I must immediately follow by saying it offers instant information about capabilities, past experience, equipment, and scheduling. All the prospect has to do is look it up on the Internet to schedule a session or check on the availability of a piece of equipment. The benefits? Saved time and instant 24-hour access.

■ ■ ■

Knowing the lay of the land is critical in prospecting for valuable natural resources. Finding exceptional customers and tailoring products to fit their needs rather than those of your business is the way successful salespeople find prospects for their businesses. In the next chapter, we look at the range of prospecting tools available to a self-employed person. These tools will help you make that initial contact that starts the sales process off and sets the tone for everything you follow with. Targeting your best prospects before you use these prospecting tools will make that first contact successful because you'll already have several valuable things in common, particularly a good match between the needs of that person and the solutions you offer.

CHAPTER 3

# PROSPECTING
# TOOLS

$K$nowing who your prospects are is the first step in prospecting. Preparing your products to satisfy those customers is the second step. Making contact with those prospects and setting a time to make your sales presentation is the third step in the prospecting process. It is also the hardest step for many self-employed people because it involves contacting people you don't know personally and soliciting their interest in what you do. Making contact is often so frightening that many of us do everything we can to avoid it. This fear is probably the number one reason why many self-employed people either fail or get stuck at one income level. Without new customers, any business will have problems as old customers move on or cease to need your services. This process of attrition is one reason why you must market and sell yourself constantly. The other compelling reason for making sales a regular aspect of your business is growth.

Growth not only improves your potential for profit, it can mean more interesting work, more choices, and a more flexible approach to what you do. Even if you're incredibly busy now, you can be better off with a higher level of work or work that involves a more interesting and specialized aspect of what you do. To accomplish these goals, you must find new customers.

## THE PROSPECTING PROCESS

If you have never prospected for new, previously unknown customers, it may seem an overwhelming task. But if you understand that task as a series of simple steps, then it becomes a much easier (and friendlier) situation. Knowing and understanding the underlying process makes even the most complex subject clear, and selling yourself is no exception.

Prospecting requires a series of actions that I'll be going over in the next few chapters. For now, let's look at the process. It goes something like this:

- *Step One:* Identify your best customers and create a demographic profile of common traits.
- *Step Two:* Identify interest groups or other sets of people who share those traits. For instance, a kitchen designer might focus on local people

who subscribe to design magazines, live in certain suburbs, and have household incomes of $80,000+.

■ *Step Three:* Make a list of actual customers. In the previous example, a call to a list broker could result in a list of people who fit all these criteria. The broker can acquire a list of subscribers to certain magazines organized by ZIP code and cross-reference it with other demographic data to create a custom list of prequalified prospects. You can find list brokers in the Yellow Pages under Mailing Lists. You can also get similar demographic lists on CD-ROM. The lists should include phone numbers, addresses, and other information.

■ *Step Four:* Determine ways to reach your desirable potential customers. You've got names, addresses, and phone numbers. You can use the phone, direct mail, advertising in publications they read, and so on.

■ *Step Five:* Plan a series of contacts with the members of your list. These contacts might include a letter of introduction, a phone call seeking an appointment, a survey, an invitation to an event like a seminar or class, a series of postcards, ads, and so on. You must use an ongoing series—it usually takes numerous contacts before a prospect decides to go further. This series of contacts builds trust.

- *Step Six:* Make contact personally—that is, phone and set an appointment to meet, or run ads designed to bring people into your store or office so they make contact with you.
- *Step Seven:* Start the selling process to turn prospects into customers.

These steps show up in more detail in the next chapters and throughout Section Two of *Sales for the Self-Employed*. But before you can take each step, you need something else to get through the process: tools. Like a prospector with compass, pick, and mule, you need a range of tools and the skills to use them to their full potential. Your prospecting tools include many already mentioned—phone, computer, advertising, direct mail—plus a host of others. In this chapter, we take a quick look at some of the essential tools for successful business prospecting. For a much more comprehensive look at these tools and more, read *Marketing for the Self-Employed,* our companion volume in this series.

## THE TOOLKIT

These are the basic marketing and prospecting tools that every self-employed person should develop at least a working familiarity with. Some may be beyond the scope of your business or simply not suitable. Others may not be cost-effective or may not be suitable for more than small-scale use. Some may prove so effective that you have little need for the others. And you may find yourself much more comfortable with some while others turn you off. A word of advice, though: Don't automatically eliminate a tool because of initial personal discomfort. These are often the most effective tools you can use, and the discomfort will disappear as you begin to discover that effectiveness. There is nothing like a little success to make a once-fearsome action seem a lot more inviting.

## The Phone

You should learn to love the phone. It is cheap, personal, direct, and instantaneous. The phone is, in my opinion, the single most effective marketing and sales tool for self-employed people. Yet it also causes a level of fear second only to public speaking. It seems easy enough. You pick up the phone, dial prospective customers, and ask for an appointment. They either say yes or no. You make your appointment or thank them for their time and make the next call. It costs virtually nothing in comparison to almost any other technique, and its results are instantaneous. So why don't we all use the phone to its full marketing potential?

It has to do with the concept of *cold calling*. We call calls like these *cold* because they involve making unsolicited approaches directly to a customer. And if you take the boiler-room approach of simply calling every Sam, Dick, and Mary, you'll get a frosty reception much of the time. There are several skills involved in prospecting with a phone. First, you must know something about the people you are calling. The more the better. Otherwise you're wasting their time, and nothing turns people off faster than that. Second, you must use a script to get appointments. The idea of using a script seems to shock a lot of people—it seems as though you're using a canned presentation to sell your very personal business.

The script is nothing more than a step-by-step guide to make sure you say what you want and keep the conversation moving toward your goal of getting an appointment. The selling side of the script might read like this:

"This is Martin Edic calling for Bill Johnson."

"I'm with the Concept Company."

"Mr. Johnson, I wonder if you have a few minutes? I'd like to talk to you about the effectiveness of your marketing. Yes, we're a consulting group—we help companies like yours evaluate the effectiveness of their marketing budget. Can we get together so I can show you what we do? Great, is Monday at 10:30 OK? How about Tuesday afternoon?"

"Thanks again for your time. I'll see you on Tuesday."

This helps keep you on track. There are a couple of important things happening here. First, your primary goal is to get an appointment. Don't talk about your business or rattle on about past experience, special tools, or anything else. Just go for the appointment. If they ask you to send information, just tell them that every situation is different and that you'd like to show them personally how you can help them. And always offer a specific date and time with an alternate ready if it won't work.

Scripts are a real help for the fear that often accompanies calling. Just keep moving through the script. If someone has no interest, say thank you, hang up, and immediately dial the next number. The refusal has nothing to do with you if you have been brief and polite. If you get a rude brush-off, it is likely that something you know nothing about is behind it—don't take it personally.

There is a simple routine that helps turn cold calls into warm calls. It's a motivation game. Just realize that if it takes ten calls to make an appointment and three appointments to make a sale that generates $300 in profits, each call was worth $10! At ten bucks each, a few rejections can still seem like money in the bank. And it's likely that you will do much better than this if you've prequalified your prospects and assembled a highly motivated list.

## One-Sentence Description

You may have noticed that the caller in the script quickly described his business in one sentence: "We help companies like yours evaluate the effectiveness of their marketing budget." Can you describe what you do, in a benefit-oriented manner, in one sentence? For my money, developing a great one-sentence description of your business is better than a flashy brochure or expensive ad. And even if you need those brochures and ads, your one-sentence description can serve as the hook they use to pull in customers. Best of all, it costs nothing to come up with one.

It will be a challenge to boil down what you do to a few words, especially because you are so personally involved in every aspect of your business. Ask friends and customers how they would describe it. You may be surprised at what you hear. Look for action and benefit-oriented words that convey a sense of real-world effectiveness. In my example, those words are *help, companies like yours, evaluate, effectiveness,* and *budget* (almost the whole sentence is action words!). They promise results and address key issues like budgets and expert assistance.

Once you've developed a simple description, try it out on people whenever someone asks what you do. Mess around with the wording until it rolls easily off the tongue at the drop of a hat. Keep it simple and use it all the time. It's free!

## Business Name

Your business name should be easy to remember, easy to pronounce, and descriptive without being generic. As easy as that all sounds, large companies spend millions developing unique, marketable names because they realize what a powerful asset a recognized and respected name is. You must do the same. As a very personalized business, self-employment is almost completely a relationship-driven thing: Your name and reputation are inextricably linked. You can use your own name with a descriptive tag line—say, Marilyn Rose, Medical Writer—if it fits the criteria of pronounceability and memorability. If your name is very unusual or hard to pronounce, consider using a company name that will be easier for your customers to say and remember.

## Logo

A logo is a visual symbol of your business. Logos were originally developed because most customers were illiterate. A wheelwright used a hanging wheel for a sign or logo, a blacksmith an anvil, and so on. Today, logos are equally important because we know that as many as 50 percent of us think primarily in pictures. These visual thinkers remember and represent things subconsciously in images, and a strong image has much more resonance with them than a set of words that must be represented aurally in the mind. Have a simple, effective logo designed by a good graphic designer and use it on your marketing materials.

## Business Cards

Business cards are remarkably powerful tools in the sales process. They contain all the information a prospect needs to contact you at any time. They're small enough to fit in a wallet or rotary file, yet they can be visually memorable if well designed. You can write notes on the back or even offer a mini-brochure listing a few benefits of your business. Handing them out to people usually results in them giving you theirs, establishing permission for you to contact them.

Again, have a graphic designer do your cards and have them printed on high-quality stock by a reputable printer. Your designer can handle the printing. Cheap generic cards or laser printed cards are fine for temporary use, but you do not want to convey a sense of being temporary—get good ones as soon as possible. You don't want to scrimp here because these little contact makers are often the only reminder a prospect may keep of you and your business.

Your primary goal after getting a new batch of cards should be to get rid of them. Hand them out at the drop of a hat. Attach them to all outgoing mail including bill payments, invoices, letters, and so on, even if you know the recipient already has one. Don't worry if your targets seem to have no connection with your business. They may know someone who does. I have a friend who went to a party for a college buddy at a run-down house. While there, he got talking to another guest who was a relative of the hosts. After chatting, they exchanged cards; he didn't really look at the one he got because it seemed an unlikely place to make a business connection. When he got home and emptied his pockets, he discovered he'd been talking to the

CEO of a Fortune 500 company! Needless to say, it was a good connection.

## Brochures

Everybody seems to want a brochure. Yet I often wonder if they are as effective as they should be. Many times a request for a brochure during a sales call is a signal of a brush-off. Brochures are effective tools if you use them effectively. They serve as a central information piece for your business, another contact in a series, and a way to give your customers something to read when they have nothing better to do. If you have a service that requires explanation or a product that has many relevant features and specifications, by all means have a brochure done by professionals. Otherwise, consider using the money for something more effective.

My reservations about brochures are strictly based on a sales perspective. From a marketing point of view, there may be many reasons to do one. In the sales process, however, they can interrupt the flow of a presentation or divert the customer's attention while you are gathering vital information. Don't rely too heavily on brochures as selling tools.

## Portfolio

Rather than a brochure, most self-employed people will do better with a portfolio of their work. Portfolios are easy to keep up to date, and you can customize them to fit the customer's interests during a sales presentation.

Because portfolios are such important tools for the self-employed, I cover them in detail in Chapter 12.

## Direct Mail

Why is direct mail different from regular mail? Because it is designed to be a direct-response marketing tool. Direct-response marketing goes directly to prospects and asks them to take direct action, either by picking up a phone or returning a mailer. It has an offer and a response mechanism. For a sales campaign, the offer is something of value, usually the benefit of buying your product. The call to action is to set up an appointment or other opportunity for you to make your sales presentation.

Direct mail has less obvious uses that fit well with many self-employed businesses. It serves as one more contact. It conveys information via a newsletter, personal letter, or informational article or report. It supports other tools like calls or ads. And it is an inexpensive way to maintain contact as you work your way toward that personal meeting.

Your direct mail may include postcards, sales letters, invitations, greeting cards, brochures, and anything else you send. Make sure you present your message in a professional manner that stresses the benefits to the customer of doing business with you. I strongly recommend having these pieces professionally written and designed by a graphic designer experienced in conveying information that sells. And make sure it is very easy to contact you via 800 numbers, voice mail, e-mail, reply cards, and any other method likely to be effective with your prospective customers. Send a piece to everyone on your list every month or two and follow up with calls.

## Publicity

It is amazing what the effect of even a small amount of publicity can be. People you don't know recognize your name. You get requests for information out of the blue. Doors may open that were closed previously. Your overall credibility is enhanced. This is because we still have an almost reverent belief in what we read and see on the news. The irony is that public relations professionals know that as much as 90 percent of the news starts with the efforts of publicity pros. Editors and producers in the media have an insatiable hunger for more content. Every day or every month they must start over with a blank page or a block of dead air and fill it with interesting, stimulating information for their audiences. You can be a source for that information.

When you do or participate in something newsworthy, you should tell the press. What is newsworthy? Anything that involves the interest of the readers of that publication or the audience of that show. You need an interesting angle, recognizable names, unusual products or experiences, and a good story—that is, an uplifting or thought-provoking story. While this may seem impossible to someone running an apparently mundane business, remember your story doesn't have to appeal to the general public, it only needs to appeal to people with an interest in what you do: your customers and prospects. If you're in a very specialized business, aim your press releases at trade magazines, newsletters, and other industry media. Or come up with a story explaining your unusual business to the general public.

This involves having an angle. An attorney I know who is a corporate litigator recently received extensive coverage about himself in the local business paper. Its main focus was his activities as a well-respected children's music performer with several CDs to his credit. But the angle was "lawyer plays children's music," and much of the article was information about his business.

Simple publicity is rewarding because it costs little and has a broad impact on your sales. There are many books that tell how to put together a simple press kit, write a press release, and do effective interviews. The time spent learning the ropes of publicity can be invaluable when you make one of those cold calls and the recipient says, "I just read about you in the paper." Just make sure the exposure is positive. Unless you're a rock star or a politician of a certain stripe, the old saw about any publicity being good publicity just isn't true.

### Advertising

Advertising is a powerful tool. So is a chainsaw. Used effectively, they can both get a lot of work done in a small amount of time, but used carelessly they can be costly.

Advertising, to be effective, must be well planned, well executed, consistent, frequent, and targeted at the right audience. For a self-employed person who may not need large numbers of prospects to prosper, it may be overkill. If you run a business that requires a steady stream of new customers to survive, then you must advertise. Otherwise, look carefully at other options.

Rather than randomly running ads here and there in various places, you should pick one or two media you know your customers look at and run a small but well-written and well-designed ad. This ad should run all the time, every week or month, forever, if it gets results after the first eight or nine placements. Frequency and consistency are the two attributes your advertising needs to succeed—savvy consumers develop trust and recognition gradually. We seldom respond to an ad we see once.

For a self-employed business, I recommend small display or classified ads that appear regularly and invite the prospect to call for information. These prospecting ads are not designed to build brand awareness or a company image. They are tools for finding motivated prospects for your sales efforts. Try buying a couple of months of weekly ads in the trade magazines or papers aimed at your target audience. Run a similar message in every one and make sure you always ask any callers how they heard of you. If the ad doesn't pull after 8 to 10 repetitions, try another message or medium. But give them time before you pull out.

## Networking

I've stressed the importance of building personal relationships for self-employed people. Nothing has a stronger effect than getting out and pressing the flesh and meeting people. Networking is nothing more than meeting potential prospects on neutral territory. The most important thing I can say about networking is to make sure you network where the customers are. As obvious as it seems, too many of us attend meetings of trade groups who do what we do. In other words—meetings of our competition. While it can be fun to talk shop, it doesn't get you in touch with customers. You must go where they are likely to be.

As a writer, I could attend the many writers' conferences around the country that promise to help me meet editors and agents. However, I'd be there with a lot of other writers vying for the attention of the harried editors who got talked into these little junkets. Wouldn't I be better off at a convention of editors, agents, or publishers? When you attend networking opportunities, make sure there is a likelihood that most of the attendees are good prospects for what you do. Then you can go and talk shop. I guarantee you'll get inquiries about your business in the process. Exchange cards and follow up with a sales call.

■ ■ ■

These are just a few of the prospecting tools available. By now, you know that they are actually marketing tools designed to get you in contact with potential customers. The more you learn about the marketing process, the easier the sales process will become as you focus your efforts on the most motivated prospects you can find for your specific business.

Once you have the tools and start to use them, you start to make contacts. How you handle these initial exploratory meetings is very important to the entire process. First contact is the subject of the next chapter.

# CHAPTER 4

# FIRST
# CONTACT

Learning who your best potential customers are, where you can find them, and how to use the necessary tools to reach them is only the beginning. And for many of us, this research and skill development is easier than what is yet to come: actual contact with these prospects. The research is easier because first contact has a potential for failure and the sense of fear and rejection that may accompany it. Coping with this fear is a vital aspect of learning to sell. It is such an important part of the sales process that I deal with it throughout the book and in its own chapter later in this first section. For now, let's look at a step in the sales process that has to happen before any selling can occur.

We don't live or work in a vacuum. Our labors are a part of the whole interaction of community that makes our social system function. These labors are physical, economic, intellectual, intuitive, and creative. And they always involve some kind of interaction with others, whether we are a solitary artist in a studio or a member of a team working on a manufacturing or design project. The artist has an audience, benefactors, critics, market, and resources for everything from supplies to the building he or she works in. And even if the team member is an outsider, brought in for specialized skills and experience, the links to others are obvious.

This ongoing connection to others in the work world is something that some self-employed people don't experience as much as employees do—most employees go to work each day knowing that there are others they'll see or speak with. As a writer, I often spend a work day without ever making contact with anyone else. Yet other times I am in touch with editors, sources, readers, and a host of other people. Without that contact, I wouldn't be working or earning a living.

As obvious as all this seems, I often get the impression that many self-employed people wish they could avoid going out and meeting people to generate new business for themselves. They want a magic marketing bullet that will bring the business in without a personal commitment from themselves. In the process, they spend thousands on brochures, direct mail, and advertising when they could often prosper by simply making a few phone calls. This is so common that I find it to be the norm rather than the exception, especially with neophyte self-employed people. They're very comfortable with the actual work they do and very uncomfortable with the rest of what it takes to succeed in business.

## Your Personal Investment

Which brings me to the point of this chapter and, to a great extent, this book: *You cannot sell without making a personal investment in the process.* This personal investment is your bread-and-butter product, the stock in trade of every self-employed person. You're not selling widgets or expertise; you're selling yourself as a human being. People buy your services because of who you are rather than what you are. It's personal.

So what is a personal investment and why is it so vital? It's vital because it shows your prospective customer that you have enough commitment to your business to put your reputation on the line, every day, on every job—and for them, personally. A personal investment is your focused, attentive, respectful participation in what you're selling and doing for your customers. Ninety percent of the time, if they believe that you are committed, they will hire you or buy your product. If you let them sense even a slight wavering in your commitment, you'll lose them.

## Their Personal Investment

The reason all of this is so important is that your customer is making an investment in you. They're investing time, energy, and cold, hard cash in someone who until recently was a stranger. They're taking a risk—and most of us are risk averse, especially when it comes to our jobs and our livelihoods. A big part of selling is risk aversion for both parties, creating a balance that re-assures each side that they are safe and are making the right choice.

There is another aspect to the personal investment being made by your customers. You should constantly be aware of the degree of investment they are making as you go through the selling process. Each time you speak, interact, and spend time together their invest-ment grows. At some point it becomes large enough to affect their thinking because they want something from their investment. They want a return, and pulling out will leave them empty-handed.

This desire to realize something from the invest-ment the buyer has made in time and energy is a powerful selling tool, particularly when you're making that important first contact. Take a look at the follow-ing example of Joan:

> Joan sells industrial equipment as an independent sales rep. She is not a beginner; she is very aware of what she is doing each step of the way as she contacts a prospective customer, sets up an ap-pointment, and gets together to begin the sales process. She cold calls the owners and presidents

of small manufacturing firms all over the country. Before she picks up the phone, she does a lot of homework. She knows their names, their products and customers, and the machines they have now. She knows mutual business acquaintances, and she participates in industry conferences and trade shows. All of this has one goal: To make her first contact a profitable one both for her *and* for her prospect.

When she started out, her cold calls were more like frosty calls. She knew little about the business, and no one had any idea who she was. She seldom got through to her prospects and suffered enough personal rejection to consider a different career. First contact was so difficult that after a day of people saying no, she experienced cold fear just thinking of picking up the phone to call a stranger.

Around her she saw other reps making really good money without the level of stress she was experiencing. In fact, they seemed to know everyone or at least have common ground with everyone they called. She began to realize that her first contacts would be a lot easier if she could find her own common ground with her prospects. Using the tools and concepts we've looked at in these first chapters, she began to get to know her typical prospects, to understand what motivated them—and, equally important, what

*(continues)*

turned them off. It was this negative input that really helped her achieve success.

Joan found out that the company managers she called were very busy and had little patience with salespeople who didn't understand their business. They weren't intentionally rude and abrupt; they simply didn't feel that it was their job to teach a young salesperson the ropes. Their rejection of her was based on their situation and had little to do with her personally. They simply did not want to invest time in her.

Once she understood that she had to bring something valuable to the relationship right from the start, she changed her approach and changed her success rate as a result. What she brought was a willingness to get answers for people, to convey their interests and concerns to the designers who made the machines she sold, and she always used personal references. These personal references were hard to come by at first; but as she developed satisfied customer relationships, she simply asked them to recommend her.

Joan's initial failure could have resulted in her giving up self-employment. Instead, she used it as an opportunity to learn, an essential skill for anyone who is self-employed and an essential part of sales. Gathering information is one of the primary skills of selling and is particularly important before making first contact.

Your first contact with a prospect has one objective, whether that contact is over the phone, via e-mail, or in person: to set up an appointment to make your sales presentation. This should be your overriding goal when first meeting someone. In my opinion, if you are contacting this person in the hope of doing business with him or her, an appointment should be your only target. You should not start selling or talk about your product or experiences, drop too many names or brag about your accomplishments, or rattle on nervously. Nor should you send out a brochure when asked. This is typically a polite way for the customer to end the conversation. You should:

- Be concise and brief. Don't waste time. Get to the point.
- Speak in terms of their interests, their concerns, their desires.
- Use your one-sentence, benefit-oriented description of what you have to offer.
- Tell them where you got their names, giving a specific personal reference whenever possible. If you got them from a list, you can say that your research identified them as someone with a specific need for your services.
- Ask for a meeting to show them how you can help them.

- Offer them a choice of two specific dates and times. If they cannot make either, have another specific time ready.
- Always offer actual times. Don't say: What works for you? Control the situation.
- If they show no interest at all, don't push. Ask again for the opportunity to show them your product—and if they firmly restate their lack of interest, thank them and go on to a new prospect.

## FRIENDLY ALIENS

In science fiction stories, first contact with an alien race is a favorite subject because it represents the ultimate unknown: reaching out and interacting with strange beings who may be very unlike ourselves. They may be unfriendly or even dangerous in ways we cannot predict. For the self-employed person making first contact with prospects, you can assume there is a very good probability that your aliens will be friendly. In fact, you probably have much in common. All you have to do is identify this common ground and use it to establish a bond.

Because you are both in business, you have one bond. Because there is a connection between your business and theirs (or you shouldn't be calling them!), you have another bond. These basic connections are a start. However, common ground turns up in the most

unusual places. It is part of the fascination I
the sales process that you find unusual com...
with the most unlikely prospects. Perhaps you grew up
near each other, have mutual friends, live in the same
kind of house, or share unusual hobbies. During an introductory get-together for a writing project, I sat in a
lunch meeting with an attorney friend, a venture capi-
talist, and the CEO of a midsized company. Somehow
we discovered that all of us had played in rock bands at
one point or another in our lives! This unusual connection put us all on an equal level for a few minutes
and established a bond that made the rest of the meeting a much more relaxed affair.

## Networking

As we've seen, networking is a valuable sales tool. It is
also a typical place where first contact occurs with a
stranger who may be a prospect. If you've been in business for any time at all, you've probably found yourself
at some kind of networking event. These meetings,
seminars, conferences, and dinners often have the guise
of being educational or aimed at a specific purpose, but
the true underlying intent is to bring people together
to do business.

Unfortunately, networking turned into such a
business buzzword that these events soon started to follow an uncomfortable format where people seem to
have a card at hand and think that merely by being
there they will find business. I generally stay away from

events specifically organized for networking because they usually draw crowds of insurance salespeople and other sales pros whose only reason for being there is to sell. Your success as a networker is directly related to what events you attend and how you handle them. As we discovered in Chapter 3, successful networking starts by going where the customers are, that is, attending events aimed at a target group of prospects. But what do you do to turn these events into successful first contact situations? Start by thinking like a counselor or therapist. This means doing some creative listening.

## Creative Listening

Creative listening is a simple technique that many of us find very difficult to pull off. Imagine you are a therapist about to see a new patient. The patient will be nervous and unsure, and it is your job to put him at ease and make it easy for him to communicate with you.

He walks in and you say hello. Now you have a choice. You can start talking about what you do, or you can ask a simple question that helps him start talking. Obviously, as a therapist, your job is to help communicate his problems and begin to resolve them, so you'll want to get him talking. The same goes for you as a networker. You must get your new acquaintances talking and then do a little creative listening.

Just ask an opening question, let them respond, and then ask simple questions that keep things going. Creative listening does not involve any actual conversation on your part unless your prospects ask direct questions. Then you answer briefly and redirect your questioning to them. Most of the time they'll be more than happy to keep talking. And as they do, they're making a personal investment in you.

It's amazing how this works. I've had many conversations where I sat virtually silent while a perfect stranger poured out the story of his life and business to me. All I did was toss in an occasional question, as much to show my continuing interest as anything else. And at the end of the conversation, he inevitably said, "It's been really great talking to you. I've really enjoyed the conversation." The funny thing is that I wasn't conversing, just listening.

There's no secret here. You just stop your internal dialogue—the one that wants to interrupt, tell stories, correct mistakes, and so on—and listen. Really listen. You'll find out incredible amounts of information about prospects that you can use to make an appointment when you call them later. And, because they have made a significant personal investment in you, they'll be receptive to that call when it comes.

## PROFESSIONAL COMMUNICATOR

Salespeople, much like therapists, are professional communicators. We listen attentively and process the information we receive to find the most important things that we're hearing. These things are problems, challenges, requests for help or information, and sources for future business. Once we've found out some of these important things, we address them as part of the sales process and offer solutions, resources, and advice that helps the prospect. As part of this process, we sell what we do for a reasonable consideration. First contact is the first personal step in this professional communications process. It establishes the beginning of a bond of trust—and like a therapeutic relationship, it entails great responsibility. We cannot lie, promise things we can't deliver, or fail to follow up without disrupting the relationship—probably forever.

■ ■ ■

First contact is simple if you're prepared. It is a lot easier to call or contact strangers when you know a lot about them. Do your homework and you'll get through the door for that first real selling opportunity: the appointment.

# CHAPTER 5

# THE
# APPOINTMENT

Do you remember the first time you sat down and talked to a potential customer about your work? Perhaps that has yet to happen. Either way, you know it is an exciting and nerve-racking prospect. You want the business. You're sure of yourself and unsure of yourself. You don't know a lot about what your prospects want or why they asked you to meet with them. These questions probably roll around in your head from the time you agree upon a meeting until you're actually face to face, with a time period specifically set aside to discuss your relationship.

In Section Two, we look at the first part of the sales process in detail, including preparing your presentation and going through the actual meet-and-greet step that starts it off on the right or wrong foot. In this brief chapter, we look at your mental preparation and  see why getting the ground rules right before you meet is vital—even if you're the only player who knows them.

## A DESIGNATED TIME SLOT

If you're a good time manager, you know the power of setting aside certain time periods for specific tasks. You mark an event in your calendar and when the time arrives, you focus your undivided attention on that event. This focus and attentiveness make it possible to get a lot more effective things accomplished because you can bring your full faculties to bear on them.

When you set up an appointment or meeting to start the sales process, try to have that time dedicated solely to the business at hand. Tell the prospect that you're doing so. Say, "We'll need 30 minutes to cover what we both need to know to decide whether to go further," or "Can we block out a half hour to go over how I can help you out?" The important thing is to try to make clear that this time period is dedicated to your business together and nothing else.

The sales process is a fluid exchange of information and requires continuity and attention to keep flowing. Frequent interruptions, no matter how trivial, disrupt the process and break down the communications flow. For this reason, you may want to schedule meetings at the beginning or end of the business day or away from the ebb and flow of the prospect's daily work. If the prospect is coming to you at your office, shop, or workplace, set aside an uninterrupted period of time for that meeting. Turn on the voice mail, don't schedule any other meetings, and give the gift of your undivided attention.

## YOUR UNDIVIDED ATTENTION

This gift of undivided attention represents a measurable personal investment on your behalf and will often be rewarded. We all like to feel important, and nothing helps the sales process more than to walk away from a sales meeting with the feeling that the other party is really interested in helping us resolve our problems. This investment on your part builds your customer's self-esteem—and there are few more valuable gifts you can offer.

## PREPARATION

The only way to get right down to business and really make progress in a brief meeting is by being fully prepared. This preparation includes:

- *Customer research:* Go out and find out as much as you can about their business. Ask business acquaintances, go to the library and look up articles about them, check with business associations. This is both a background check to warn you of potential problems and an information-gathering process. It really helps when customers see you've done your homework.

- *Portfolio and presentation preparation:* We cover this is Section Two, but for now you should be aware that you must customize your presentation to the needs of each customer and you should do it ahead of time.
- *Rehearsal:* Go over your presentation either mentally or with a partner to make sure you cover all the points. Use notes if necessary. A rehearsal is a powerful tool for making your presentation sing.
- *Call to confirm:* Always call that morning or the day before to confirm that you're still on. You can talk with an assistant, secretary, or other gatekeeper who has access to your prospect's schedule. It saves time and serves as a reminder that you're coming in.

Preparation also includes dealing with stage fright. Stage fright is a common affliction and, to a certain degree, is a healthy indication of getting yourself keyed up for the event. Carried too far, it can serve as an excuse to avoid selling. Stage fright recedes with experience and preparation. If you lack experience, make up for it by preparing carefully and rehearsing. And remember what the manager told me the first time I got on stage at a crowded nightclub with my first band: Everybody gets it—but once you get started, it goes away. This is true if you prepared well.

## LONG-DISTANCE SELLING

You won't always sell at face-to-face meetings. Often you'll work over the phone, via e-mail or snail mail, or through intermediaries. These media have the advantage of being fast and the disadvantage of not allowing you to react to nonverbal signals.

Selling on the phone involves the same process as any other selling although it may be compressed somewhat. You must meet, qualify, and present, and you must ask for the sale or close. You can use a script or notes spread out before you and take notes as you go to give you a good handle on how well you're doing.

Selling through others is potentially dangerous as you cannot control how they represent you to the customer. If an intermediary sets you up to do business with someone, don't assume it's a done deal: Go into the first business step treating it as a part of the sales process in which your goal is to determine what your intermediary has promised or agreed to. You must clarify these issues yourself with the customer before you go further.

Selling in a store? The process may only take a few minutes, but you should still go through it. You still need to know why the customers are there and what problems they are seeking resolutions for, and you must explain how you can solve those problems. It may happen in a few sentences, but it is still the same sales process.

I've sold projects via e-mail, and it can be a great presales medium. However, you'll still need personal contact of some sort and, again, the process is the same. Be sure to save your e-mail correspondence as you go through the process. It will be valuable if any disputes or confusion arise later.

## PROPOSALS, ESTIMATES, AND QUOTES

Often, after an initial meeting, the customer will ask you for a proposal, quote, or estimate to take the sales process to the next step. If this is the case, you must determine exactly what the proposal or quote should contain. Many companies have standard formats they want vendors or content providers to use, and you must follow them. A nonstandard presentation may mean automatic rejection by various corporate bureaucrats.

Make sure you use the appointment to gather as much information as possible for the proposal you'll be preparing so you can address the specific problems your customer is most concerned about. Again, by carefully going through the qualifying process, you'll be able to address every hot button issue in your proposal. This kind of specific problem-solving approach often helps you get past the lowball quotes and inexperienced but cheap competition.

## ENDING THE MEETING

Try to be the one who ends the meeting. Say that you've got all the information you need and that you'll either get back to them or that you can handle the work (if that's the case). Quickly review what you've learned with the customer and ask if you've covered everything. Arrange the next meeting if necessary or a start date for the work and thank the customer for her time.

By taking control at the end you make life a lot easier for customers. They don't have to kick you out or cut you off. And it shows that both you and they have busy lives and that you respect that.

## REVIEW AND FOLLOW-UP

After the appointment, it is very important to schedule a review period with yourself. Think about what you accomplished or what you missed and try to identify what worked and what didn't. Make notes in your customer file and use them later. If you left out a question or need a little more information, simply call and ask for it. Say, "I was going over my notes and I realized that I still wasn't clear on. . . ."

Always follow up with a personal note thanking customers for their time. If you're doing business together, tell them you look forward to working together. If you're not, tell them you hope to in the future. These follow-up notes generate future business, turn negative meetings around, and generate referrals. They are vital. And your competition probably never sends them.

As a self-employed person, I've come to really look forward to initial appointments with prospective customers because I never know what to expect. The appointment may mean meeting an interesting person and taking on a new and exciting project. It may mean learning that someone has recommended me or that somehow word of my work has preceded me, both events telling me that my own marketing works. Whether the meeting results in business or not, I always learn something interesting.

## SAYING NO

Even a very negative experience can have a strong positive impact on your business knowledge and confidence. With success comes the valued ability to say no to work that you have a bad feeling about. Even the hungry newcomer needs to learn and exercise this important confidence-builder. Turning down work often enhances your desirability in the eyes of others because of a quirk of human nature that makes us want what we can't have. Once you've decided not to take on a project, trust your feelings and don't give in to offers of higher payment or improved control. The underlying reason for not taking the job still exists. Be polite but firm and express the hope that at some future time you can work together on a different kind of project.

■ ■ ■

As you've discovered in these chapters, I believe that preparation is what makes both prospecting for new customers and selling to those prospects possible. Sales involves all kinds of preparation from basic research to mental rehearsal and skills development. In Chapter 6, we look at formal sales training and other skill-building processes that you should be incorporating into your overall business abilities.

# CHAPTER 6

# TRAINING

# YOURSELF

As a self-employed person, you will always be selling. Sales is not a discrete part of running your business; it runs through everything you do from casual conversation to working on the details of a big job. Those conversations and that attention to detail send an ongoing message to your market about you and how you do business. That message has a direct and powerful effect on how easy it is to sell your product.

You can deal with this integration of selling into every aspect of your business in either of two ways. You can pretend it's not happening and continue as you have, letting your work speak for itself. We'll call this subconscious selling—your conscious mind has decided to leave sales to the subconscious. The other way is to develop an awareness of the sales component in everything you do and work to improve it. This conscious approach means putting the importance of selling up there with what you think of as the real work you do.

## SUBCONSCIOUS SELLING

Subconscious selling is not necessarily a bad thing. If you harbor deep-seated prejudices about the propriety of tooting your own horn in public or merely feel a distaste for sales, then subconscious selling may be your only choice. The problem with choosing to say "I am not a salesperson, I am a [whatever-you-do]" is that you still need to sell to survive but you've relegated this important survival skill to a part of you that isn't always under control. As a result, you may lose opportunities or find yourself making inappropriate sales pitches at the wrong times.

These prejudices and fears regarding sales are common but often groundless, being based more in our upbringing than any real experience. Coping with them by ignoring them may mean missing out on what is really a fascinating aspect of being self-employed. Learning to sell means developing an incredibly useful skill, one that you can carry to any job, in any location, under any circumstances. Because sales is really the study of human nature and the way we communicate, it is a subject that can be very enlightening if you embrace it.

## CONSCIOUS SELLING

To experience this enlightenment, you need to consciously make the decision to learn sales as a challenging skill. This includes activities like reading books and articles about it, attending and participating in training, observing the sales process as practiced by others, and taking a real interest in the process.

Learning a skill is different from learning information or facts. We learn skills through hands-on experience combined with teaching. Skill learning is a truly interactive process because humans don't just learn on an intellectual basis, we learn physically. Our bodies learn how certain activities feel, smell, sound, and look as we participate in them. For instance, watching an Olympic competition has much more meaning for us if we have actually tried the sport we're watching, no matter how inept we may have been in the process. Sales is no different. Once you have consciously tried selling, going through each step and responding to a customer, your entire perception of how we interact and engage in transactions will change. Your consciousness of this aspect of human nature will be altered.

Learning to sell involves the same series of steps that all learning experiences share. We start by becoming conscious that there is an underlying process we were not aware of before. We may not have a clear understanding of how to do it, but we've started to see that it exists. Because of this awareness, we subconsciously start to observe and learn about the process, gathering information and experience without a great deal of conscious organization. This mishmash of input is the fertile soil that the learning process requires to take shape. As beginners, we fill our minds up with a bewildering amount of information that doesn't always make sense to us.

This information-gathering stage is the beginning of any learning or creative process. As confusing and disorganized as it may feel, it is a perfectly normal and acceptable way to learn. As beginners, we don't have the experience to sort the important information from the less important. All we can do is take it in and remain open-minded.

Somewhere into the process an interesting thing happens: Previously confusing events start to make sense. An order starts to emerge. We see the connections between seemingly illogical actions and information. We've left the beginner stage and have begun to have a more engaged awareness. This light of knowledge is what drives us as humans to excel. The way unconsciously gathered knowledge sorts itself out and emerges into our conscious lives is one of the great fascinations of life.

This chapter is about learning and sales. You have two choices. You can work on learning about selling and treat it as a fascinating opportunity, or you can put it on the back burner and let the knowledge force itself out over time. The first choice means embracing a part of your business that may not have an immediate appeal and trusting that it will be worth the effort. The second choice, subconscious selling, will slow you down and may mean missed opportunities.

## LEARNING

Obviously, the self-employed person with a desire to learn more about the oft-mysterious process of personal sales will get the most out of this book. You have demonstrated that interest by reading this far and sticking with me as I digress into the seemingly arcane process of learning a new skill. Now, before we go further with the factual process of selling, I'm going to suggest that you make a larger commitment to yourself and your business by finding ways to learn, hands-on, the physical skill of selling.

This real-life practice can take place as you work, in seminars and classes, through close observation of others while they sell, and through practice on willing friends, spouse, or family. It is important because of the way we as humans process information and experience.

## VISUAL, AUDITORY, KINETIC

In our minds, we represent information and experience as pictures, sounds, feelings, and to a lesser extent smells. Many of us use one of these systems as a primary representational system. People who study this sort of thing estimate that 50 percent of us think primarily in pictures while another 25 percent hear sounds and 25 percent form patterns of feelings. Our language often gives signals as to which system we prefer. We say things like: "Picture this, you're in a boat on a large blue river with trees blowing in the wind . . ." or "Imagine you're in a boat, the water lapping against the creaking wood and the wild rustle of wind all around you in the trees . . ." or ". . . the boat is bobbing in the cool current while the gentle breath of wind is coming across the tree-lined shore to ruffle your hair." Each description tells you how the person describing the scene may process information internally. I've overstated these examples for effect, but people do say things like this—and such statements tell us a lot about the people who say them. The first is primarily visual, creating a picture in the mind; the second auditory, creating a soundscape; and the third kinetic, describing the physical feeling involved in the memory.

Knowing these systems is important to any human interactive process—including sales—because they have a direct effect on how successful your communications will be. If you talk about visual images to a person who thinks in terms of sounds, you may have a communications breakdown without ever realizing why. By simply making certain that you couch your presentation in all three systems, you'll avoid any subconscious failure to communicate. We look at this full-sensory approach to sales in greater detail in Section Three.

You can learn these kinds of skills intellectually from a book, but they will not become functional until you go out into the world and practice them. The best way to accomplish this is to attend sales training sessions on a regular basis and to look for other opportunities to enhance your communications skills. These may include motivational seminars, college classes, group activities like sports teams or drama productions, personal counseling and therapy, or performance arts. In each case, you'll learn through interaction with others.

In addition to formal training, you can learn a lot by observing other salespeople at work. This is easy in our materialistic society because there is a constant flow of selling going on everywhere we go. At a fast food restaurant, suggestive selling offers every customer an additional item after they order. In a bookstore, a clerk recommends a genre novel to a customer buying a similar title. At the health club, a smiling clerk lets you know that a karate class is opening up. Your daily mail is full of sales pitches and ads, as are the media you encounter everywhere from the ride to work to relaxing in front of the tube after a long day. Instead of complaining about this barrage of selling, try to look at it critically to discover why it does or does not work.

## THE OUTSIDE PERSPECTIVE

One powerful training technique you can use is disassociation. With disassociation, you actually observe yourself in a sales situation. Anyone who has taken ski or golf lessons may have had the experience of watching themselves on videotape as they try out various techniques. This lets you step aside and see yourself, in full clumsy splendor, as you perform. Inevitably the observation leads to insights about performance. Disassociation is a similar technique. Immediately after a sales presentation, when you are reviewing your performance, try stepping away and pretending that you are reviewing a videotape of what just occurred. Instead of being there seeing through your eyes and feeling through your body, look at yourself, in your mind's eye, from an outside perspective—the proverbial fly-on-the-wall view. See yourself going through the process and try to observe how your prospect reacts and responds.

While it may seem impossible to rewind the mental tape and view it from a disassociated viewpoint, you'll find you can do it. Perhaps the ability comes from the way our subconscious records much more information than we can process in real time. Perhaps it comes from the way our imagination lets us construct a different viewpoint from the existing information we have, just as a 3-D rendering program on a computer can create a three-dimensional image from a set of coordinates. I think it is likely to be a combination of the two skills.

There are games you can play to make this observation easier. Imagine yourself seated behind a two-way mirror observing the process, or actually watching a videotape you can slow down, rewind, or fast forward. You might try projecting yourself into the customer's shoes and observing this stranger who is trying to sell you something. The ability to mentally sit in the customer's chair and try on his or her point of view would be invaluable.

## REHEARSAL

I've briefly mentioned the value of rehearsing your sales presentation. Selling is an interactive performance that involves acquiring information and input from a prospect and reacting in a positive way to that input. This performance is not a static set piece even when you're working from a script over the phone. You must tailor the products or solutions that you are selling to the needs and desires of the buyer, and your individual style will have much to do with how that buyer reacts.

Any performance benefits from rehearsal or practice. The distinction between rehearsal and practice is simple: When you practice, you are actually out there selling. When you rehearse, you are mentally preparing yourself for the practice of selling. Rehearsal is what gets you through the hard parts—the questions you can't answer or the objections you haven't prepared for. It also helps alleviate fear or stage fright because enough rehearsal can help you continue on autopilot even when your conscious mind is telling you that all is lost. This ability to finish what you start no matter how it is going is what generates the persistence that marks the work of exceptional salespeople.

There is a simple model for rehearsal that musicians use to learn and perform complex pieces of music. They first play through the sheet music and mark the spots where they stumble. Then they go through and learn these hard passages until they are second nature. By focusing on the difficult first and conquering it, the rest flows naturally and musically during performance.

Your hard spots will come in unexpected places, as you respond to unexpected combinations of problems and emotional reactions. As we go through the sales process in Section Two of *Sales for the Self-Employed,* you'll start to understand why you get in trouble at various points. These are the places where you must devise a system for coping with the problem and learn that system until it becomes automatic.

The best rehearsals are live, in real time, with a partner who takes the opposite side of the transaction. They are not always confrontational; they are supposed to be real and help you respond, on the fly, to real responses. You can work with a friend, business associate, fellow self-employed person, or family member. One of the great values in taking sales training courses is that they usually involve role-playing with other participants in the class. However you rehearse, it is important to do it with others—physical practice is what truly teaches any skill.

## PERSISTENCE

Sales professionals often list sheer persistence as the most valued sales skill. Persistence in its purest form is a double-edged sword. On one hand, it will help you stick to the path when things get tricky—but on the other it can turn off customers who feel you are pushing them into a choice they don't want.

The most effective way to build and monitor persistence in your sales efforts is to promise yourself that you'll always finish the entire sales process once you start. This doesn't mean closing every sale. You may find that a prospect is unqualified and decide that you must stop at that point. You may realize that your solution is not the optimum one for the customer's needs and bow out by offering a referral to a better resource.

However, making it a personal rule that you will, whenever possible, complete the transaction is a recipe for sales success. Your competition will always give up at some point, possibly for a good reason. You can persist till the end as long as you know your limits and predetermine parameters that tell you when to stop. These parameters may include price, terms, hostility, fear or other negative emotional response on the part of the buyer, time limitations, or whatever you choose. Set your own ground rules and stick to them until experience tells you otherwise.

■ ■ ■

Training yourself, in sales or any other skill, is a lifelong challenge. The things you learn are wide-ranging and include everything from product knowledge to the psychology and resilience of the human spirit. You meet and interact with interesting people on an almost primal level, negotiating for mutual benefit. Along the way, you learn about yourself and become a better businessperson in the process. Whether you like it or not, sales is an integral part of being in business, one that you can ignore at your peril or embrace and profit thereby.

# CHAPTER 7

# FEAR AND
# REJECTION

There are two basic kinds of motivation that help us take action and make decisions. Motivation *toward* things or events entices us to seek an alluring future benefit. Motivation *away from* things causes us to take action to avoid perceived threat or danger. While it may seem that a forward or toward motivation is a more positive and effective one, this not always the case.

When we are in the market for a car, we often feel both kinds of motivation. We want safety features like airbags and antilock brakes to protect us from crashes; we want enticing features like sporty performance, bright colors, and luxury interiors to improve the future quality of our life. From a sales point of view, both are reasonable motivations for making a purchase, and the car salesperson who addresses both will be more likely to make the sale.

Before you can understand the motivations that may help a customer buy your products, you have to look at the motivating factors that can help you become a more effective salesperson. As a person trying to convince another of the value of your work, you have both the motivation to succeed so as to move toward a better life and motivation to protect yourself from failure and the problems it will cause. These potentially conflicting motivations are part of a big problem many salespeople face: Fear.

Fear is the number one reason why we don't go out and actively promote our businesses. It causes laziness, procrastination, inability to finish things, and many other symptoms of unsuccessful selling. The fear may be of things we would never have predicted—fear of looking stupid, fear of being rejected, fear of success, fear of the unknown, and practically any kind of fear imaginable. I, for one, still shudder when I first dial the phone to make a cold call even though my experience tells me that nothing bad will happen. It is a deep-rooted fear.

So how do you cope with fear of the sales process? We've already looked at how preparation and practice can reduce the uncertainty that causes fear. And we've looked at how experience can give you tools to work past fear. In this chapter, we take a quick look at a few more tools to help you get past any fears you may have about selling and at one fear that is more common than the others, fear of rejection.

## NEGATIVE AND POSITIVE

When we talked about away-from and toward motivations, it may have seemed that we were really talking about negative and positive. But the negative motivation, in the case of a car buyer concerned about safety, can be a positive one when looked at in the overall picture. The negativity that leads to a fearful or uncontrolled situation is different. To understand it, consider something about the way our brains process information.

We tend to process positive information first. The usual example of this is my ordering you to *not* think of the color blue. Don't think of the color blue. What happened? You had to think of blue in order to negate it! Negating an action can only occur after considering the action. You must have something in mind before you can negate it.

The importance of this in the sales process is simple. Don't use negative language or actions to sell because your customers must experience every negative thing you bring up, if only subconsciously, before they can negate it. And as you build a series of negative images, sounds, or feelings, something can happen to both you and the customer: You can both start feeling bad about the process.

Does this mean that you should not use fear or negative examples in your sales presentation? No. There are many situations where you can build a negative situation and use it to motivate people away from the bad and toward your product that solves the bad thing. This works—but there is always the danger of leaving people with a vague feeling that they just made a decision based on negative reasons.

The way out of this is to always accompany a negative problem with a positive action statement about your solution or product. In fact, seeking to speak always in a positive way actually changes both your view of the sales situation and that of your customer. My own experience of this proved its power to me at a time when there was very little positive going on in my life and consequently little positive attitude on my part.

I had recently suffered a series of losses and setbacks in my personal life and was bitter and angry. Many things I had taken for granted had changed unexpectedly, and I had failed to change with them. During this time I met a new friend who, after spending some time with me, told me that she had a problem with our relationship. She said that while she often enjoyed my company, my relentless negativity was getting very hard to take. Unless I tried to develop a more positive point of view, she would go her own way.

This was a total shock to me. I'd always considered myself a positive, forward-looking person, interested in the potential of things. Now someone I respected and valued had told me the opposite—and what's more, I knew it to be true, especially when I reviewed recent conversations. I was increasingly negative, taking the pessimistic view of every event around me.

I decided to take a drastic step. I had read of the power of positive thinking, but in my cynical state I lumped it in with other New Age, touchy-feely stuff. In spite of this negative view, I decided to be relentlessly positive about everything, whether I was sincere or not. I would seek to put a positive spin on every idea, event, conversation, and story in my life, even if it was a completely phony effort. And from that point on I became almost sickeningly positive.

The results were incredible, blowing away my most skeptical beliefs. Strangers opened up to me and told me incredible stories. Old friends commented on how different I was and asked what had changed. My business turned around as clients called seemingly out of the blue. I found it was no more work to make a positive comment or criticism than it was to make a negative one, and I began to see the potential opportunity hidden in what looked like negative events.

I haven't turned into a New Ager, but I am more respectful of their interests than I was before. What I have turned into is a true believer in the power of setting positive goals and striving to reach them by taking one step after another. The moral of this little tale is that there is a direct and measurable benefit to taking the positive approach in your selling as in your life.

## GOALS

Goals are another way of eliminating or dissipating fear. A well-thought-out and well-planned goal-setting program has a remarkable way of making things happen. You create a specific goal and break down the process of achieving it into easily accomplished steps. These steps must be actions rather than philosophical or intellectual exercises. The importance of action in the sales process is directly related to the goals process: Actions cause other actions—or, as we learned in school, for each action there is an equal and opposite reaction. You step forward and something gets out of your way.

Goals and planning are so important to the sales process that I've devoted the next chapter to them. They still deserve mention here, though, because setting goals and planning their execution gives you a bigger picture. This helps you put minor or major setbacks and fears in perspective. So what if you blew the sale today? In your plan, you'll be making many sales, and one falling by the wayside means little in the bigger scheme of things.

## REJECTION

"I don't want you or your product. I'm not interested today. Quit bothering me. I already own a [whatever-it-is]. Can't you people leave me alone?"

Rejection is a tough one for anyone to handle, and there is always a certain amount of rejection involved when we ask people to make decisions, no matter how beneficial they may be. Because as self-employed people we have a lot personally invested in what we're selling, it's easy to feel each rejection as a personal attack. Rejection causes fear and fear prevents us from working at our confident best. It's a vicious cycle.

The best way out of this cycle is a remarkably simple statement consisting of only four words. Before I tell you what they are, I must give credit where credit is due. Consultant, author, and consummate observer of the self-employed life Hubert Bermont, in his classic book on self-employment, *How to Succeed as a Consultant in Your Own Field* (Prima), tells a story of having lunch with a psychiatrist friend. During the course of their conversation, the friend said he knew four words that would solve 90 percent of his clients' problems, if only his clients would take them to heart. Intrigued, Bermont pressed him for the words. They were: *don't take it personally.*

Think about it. Nearly every rejection you experience is rooted in the other person's situation. Maybe he's having a bad day. Maybe he's on the verge of bankruptcy and angry at the world. Maybe you're bald, and a bald guy just hit his car in the parking lot. The point is that it's not your fault—so don't take it personally.

The power of these four words is liberating. They don't tell you to be irresponsible or negligent; they tell you that many things others do probably don't have anything to do with you. Remember the power of personal investment? You're investing yourself personally in the interests of those you sell to. However, you cannot always predict their reaction. If it is negative, you have two choices: You can take it personally and feel hurt, rejected, or angry—or you can realize it's their problem, not yours.

■  ■  ■

Both fear and rejection are internal emotional reactions to events outside your control. To cope with these powerful emotions, you need to establish as much control over outside events as possible by setting goals, educating yourself, and gathering information prior to the sales process. And when you get involved in the process, you must understand that some things are not in your control and may reflect situations that have nothing to do with you. You are probably merely in the wrong place at the wrong time. Move on and reflect on what happened. The next time, you'll have a greater perspective and less fear going into the process.

# CHAPTER 8

# YOUR
# SALES PLAN

Because you own and run a business, selling cannot be a full-time activity. Sales is only one of the many actions you must pursue to ensure the success of your business. You have limited time and energy to put into your sales, so you must do everything you can to make the most of these assets. You must manage your time efficiently and use leverage to make sure that each action you take has the greatest possible effect.

## TIME

The selling required to keep most self-employed people busy does not require significant amounts of money. Instead, it requires that most valuable of assets, time. We all live with limited amounts of time that we must apportion out to various activities. We spend time educating ourselves, working on problems, generating business, and relaxing with our families and friends, not to mention eating and sleeping. Fitting time for a real sales effort into this packed schedule requires careful planning.

Like any other action, sales can be done two ways. You can plunge in and learn as you go. This means making many mistakes, redoing many things, and wasting large amounts of time. Or you can carefully plan a few powerful actions that will make each sales presentation have a much higher likelihood of success. This planning will take some time up front, but it will save enormous amounts of time and make your sales experience much more enjoyable and profitable.

## LEVERAGE

The reason planning makes such a big difference is leverage. Archimedes said, "Give me a long enough lever and a fulcrum to rest it on and I will move the world." You may not move the world, but with a long lever you can move your business to a higher and more profitable level. Knowledge is your fulcrum, and planning how to use that knowledge is your long lever. Planning activities are time-savers. It has been estimated that for every minute of planning you do, you save 12 minutes of time while implementing that plan. It's easy to see where the leverage comes in.

For now, as you read this book and start to use the techniques it offers, you should be putting together a simple sales plan. The hour or so per week you spend on planning and upgrading your sales strategy will make a big difference. You'll be better prepared, you'll target highly motivated prospects, you'll spend less time on dead ends, and you'll enjoy the process much more. An hour per week will save you many hours of frustration.

## WRITING YOUR SALES PLAN

A sales plan is an outline that you follow to keep your sales efforts on track. It has goals, a strategy, and a series of tactics to implement that strategy and achieve those goals. It need not be complex. For the typical self-employed person, it may only be a single page. The first plan you write will be crude, and you should count on upgrading it as your experience grows. For instance, you may find that one tactic far outperforms the others and reorient your plan to focus on that action.

Your sales plan should be in writing, even if no one but you ever sees it. Writing out a plan forces you to see it a little more objectively and, because writing in itself is an action, it starts the sales process off as soon as you put pen to paper. Projects that start with action tend to keep going, whereas projects that we mull over intellectually seldom get completed (or even started).

## A Simple Sales Plan

Let's look at the development of a simple sales plan for a consulting business. David starts his business after his old job gets downsized out of existence. He doesn't need to do any sales or marketing at first because his employer, a large aerospace company, offers him a consulting contract as part of his severance package. However, after a year of consulting with them on a more or less full-time basis, he sees the writing on the wall and recognizes that if he loses his only client, he'll be out of business. With reality setting in, he sits down and starts to plan out a strategy to gain three more solid clients over the next year.

At first, the obvious strategy is to approach other aerospace companies. On reflection and after calling a few friends, however, David realizes that there is a potential flaw in this approach. Many of these companies have experienced similar downsizing and have numerous connected ex-employees to choose from when they require help. He decides that the first part of his plan will be to identify an expert niche service that he can promote.

## Identify a Niche Market

Reviewing his experience and skills and then matching them with the ways they might be used by others leads him to a interesting realization. The most effective work he has done has involved working with subcontractors who supply parts for the large company, helping them wade through the confusing and complex process of dealing with a large company's requirements. Although he always worked for the large buyer company, he often spent most of his time with the supplier companies, and as a result had many contacts and connections among them.

David decides that his primary target group will be these smaller companies and that he will offer consultation on how to win contracts with the industry giants. His niche will be creating new markets for these companies in a rapidly changing industry.

## Make a List

David's next step is to make a list of companies and individual contacts at those companies who may be likely prospects. He starts with a directory published by a trade association and spends several evenings going through the directory to identify companies that fit some criteria he has decided may work. These criteria include product offerings, reputation, size, and profitability. He eventually has a list of 15 prospects in his database.

Once David has his hit list, he needs specific names of people to approach. He starts by calling several people at his former company and asking them for referrals. He goes to the directory he started with and gets the names of the heads of the companies and calls each company to confirm that they are still there and that he has the correct titles and spellings of their names. He finds that their assistants or secretaries are generally helpful in getting this information.

## Identify a Contact Method

List in hand, David has to decide how he will go about meeting with these prospects to arrange a simple presentation. Scanning the trade journals, he realizes that almost all of his prospects will probably be attending two major industry shows in the next three months. This becomes the basis of his contact strategy. He writes a personal letter to each explaining his business and asking if they can arrange a brief meeting during the show to discuss how he can assist them. After mailing the letters, he follows up with calls and arranges six meetings during the shows.

## Prepare the Presentation

Because these prospects are very busy and his time with them is limited, David must make a strong presentation of value to them during these meetings. He decides to prepare a brief case study of a situation where he helped a similar company get a large contract in a much shorter time frame than they had expected because of his inside knowledge. His case study focused on the time savings and the resultant profits. The case study was simple, consisting of a brief report and several charts and timelines comparing the conventional approach with his and tracking the results the two produced.

## Rehearse

Sitting down with a good friend from his former employer, he ran through his presentation several times, fine-tuning it and identifying spots where he stumbled, and streamlining it until it was relatively concise. The friend thought the resulting case study was very effective and suggested he submit it as an article to the trade magazine putting on the conference. He sent it out and received a call. They were not only printing the piece, they were offering him a chance to give a seminar on the subject. This gave him a considerable amount of extra leverage when it came to setting up meetings.

To benefit from a plan like this, you have to be willing to go through all the steps. If you do take each one and follow it to its natural conclusion, you'll find that serendipitous things will happen. In my example, the article and seminar were unexpected results of David's careful planning and preparation. This is a good example of the power of leverage and the power of actually acting on your goals.

## Sales Plan Outline

The following outline will serve as a basic guide for creating your own sales plan. Most of the information you need to create it is in this book. For more details on the many marketing tactics and skills available to self-employed people, consult the companion book to this one, *Marketing for the Self-Employed* (Prima).

DEFINE SPECIFIC SALES GOALS IN WRITING   Be specific, as in: "I want 16 new patients for my practice this year."

IDENTIFY YOUR NICHE OR SPECIALIZATION   Make sure you work from a customer-benefit point of view. It's not enough to say: "I am a computer programmer." You must say something as specific as: "I write software that helps stock analysts spot emerging markets on the Internet." This benefit-oriented approach will help you when you get to the next step.

IDENTIFY TARGET MARKETS   Your goal here is to create a list of prospects by individual person. If you've defined your niche properly, you know right where to look—for example, the niche defined in the previous step sends you after a list of stock analysts. Start a list of prospects who fit a profile of people likely to need and want your services. This list must contain several things, including specific names of individuals who have the power to make decisions and the means to pay for your work. Assembling a list of heroin addicts for a drug rehab counseling practice would be relatively easy— but assembling a list of addicts who really want to change and have the ability to pay for it would be a much greater challenge.

　　Always seek a specific person to make contact with rather than using a generic title like Buyer or CEO. We always do business with individuals, not companies. It's vital to your sales success to find the right person before you begin the sales process.

PLAN YOUR INITIAL CONTACT   Determine the best way to reach your prospects to set an appointment for your sales presentation. The most effective method is a series of contacts going from the casual to the one-on-one. This might involve a recurring ad, press coverage they are likely to see, a letter, a phone call, a referral, and finally a meeting.

PLAN YOUR PRESENTATION   How you present yourself and your products at this first meeting is vital. A poor showing seldom earns you a second chance. Plan your presentation carefully and put together a compelling one, whether it's a full-blown multimedia show, a simple portfolio, or a verbal consultation. Make it understated and professional and have a copy or some related information you can leave behind.

REHEARSE YOUR PRESENTATION   Rehearsal shows up problems, relieves stage fright, and makes a much more compelling presentation.

SCHEDULE EACH ASPECT OF YOUR PLAN   Get out a calendar and write in deadlines for completing each part of your plan and stick to them no matter what.

BUDGET THE FUNDS YOUR PLAN NEEDS   For some of us, the budget may cover a clean suit and a few lunches; for others, it may mean color brochures, multimedia presentations, and national travel expenses. Plan for these costs and set aside money on a regular basis to pay for your sales. It is a profitable investment in your future.

TAKE THE FIRST STEP   Without action, the best plans are useless. And by taking action, you change the nature of your business forever and for the better. Even if the challenge of selling yourself seems too great, just look at it as a series of easier steps that will inevitably lead you to your goal.

REVIEW, REVISE, AND REPLAY   This is an ongoing learning experience of the first magnitude. Selling yourself means presenting yourself to the world, communicating successfully with your peers, and receiving measurable input in the form of money, new business, and trust—or rejection. Don't be afraid to alter your tactics, reinforcing the ones that work well and dropping those that don't. Replay each sales session in your mind and learn from it. People will tell you fascinating things without even being aware that they are doing so. Keep your eyes, ears, and mind open.

■ ■ ■

With a simple plan for finding prospects and contacting them, you're ready to start selling. Section Two of *Sales for the Self-Employed* takes a detailed look at the process and the tools you'll learn to use as you sell yourself. Even if you never pursue a conventional sales situation, you'll learn a great deal about how we interact as human beings and how sales works as a problem-solving tool in society.

# SECTION TWO

# SELLING
# AS A PROCESS

# CHAPTER 9

# THE
# COMMUNICATIONS
# PROCESS

Our need to communicate is a primal one, one that may set us apart from many other creatures on this planet. Because of our desire and ability to communicate, we can join forces with others to accomplish things, to create, and to build. Our entire society depends on a constant series of interchanges and transactions, on the construction of networks and of the tightly knit communities and families that form our social structure. The way we communicate connects them all.

Yet many of us never spend much time considering how we communicate and how we might improve this basic skill. We take our ability to convey ideas, emotions, and memories to others for granted. In fact, many of us shy away from many forms of communication. Public speaking, once a revered art form, has become a fearsome prospect for most of us. Large numbers of students never ask questions or speak out in class because of fear of looking stupid or uncool—and thereby deprive themselves and their classmates of the exchange that makes education work. In meetings, many of us remain silent, afraid to rock the boat or state any idea that might cause a discussion.

Increasingly we learn by observation rather than by participation. Television, video, recordings, the news media, and even books like this can serve to separate us in a learning situation from others. This static, one-way model of learning has a serious flaw: It serves well to shovel facts at us but fails miserably at conveying hands-on skills. As I've noted earlier, we learn skills by doing rather than reading.

So what does all this have to do with sales and your business? In a word, everything. Very little of what we are taught in school or learn on the job working for others is useful for self-employed businesspeople trying to sell their wares. There are few formal educational opportunities to learn common-sense, real-world small business skills. As a result we have to plunge in and learn on the streets, day to day, while trying to earn a living.

If you want to learn how to sell while in school, I'd recommend taking some very different courses from the ones aimed at business majors. I'd point you at acting classes, music, advertising production, public speaking, and other role-playing courses. I'd also suggest you get a part-time job in a very busy store where you face as many customers as possible every hour you work. And then I'd tell you to consider all of these things practice for selling. And we'd start by looking at communications as a process to learn and enhance rather than something to take for granted.

## PROCESS AND CONTENT

All through this book, I keep referring to *process.* Process is how we learn skills that we use to design, build, market and sell things—or *content.* Content is material or results; process is action. The difference between the two is that once you've learned a process you carry that ability with you forever, whereas content is a result that either stays in the past or resides on a shelf for reuse.

In Section Two of *Sales for the Self-Employed,* we look at selling as a process that once learned can help us sell anything. As a self-employed person, you may only be interested in selling what you do. It doesn't matter. Sales is not content specific. Your accumulated sales skills will be useful for the rest of your life, no matter how your career changes. The reason for this is that selling is an advanced form of human communication, one that forces you to communicate effectively, concisely, and in real time in response to ongoing input.

The communications process is the same whether you are selling a widget or trying meet a potential spouse. You start with a personal desire or need. Someone else can fulfill that need but has needs or desires of his or her own that require resolution. If you are both able to listen to each other's needs and arrange a satisfactory exchange, then the sale will take place. If you fail to communicate effectively, it will not.

## SUCCESS WITHOUT SELLING

Failure to communicate is not the only reason a sale does not occur. You may communicate with each other exceptionally well, only to discover that your needs do not match up. In this case, no one has failed—the communication is successful, and you go on to the next likely prospect. In a perfect world or at least one that lacked the emotional landscape we inhabit, this would be fine. No one would feel inadequate or disappointed, angry or let down. However, as emotional creatures we have a more complex response to our attempted transactions.

How many times has the unavailability of something increased its value in your eyes? Rarity conveys value. How many times has anger or frustration served to spur you on to achieve more than you aimed at originally? Adversity motivates. How many times have you gone back to the drawing board and sought a new approach to resolve a problem? Failure is experience. And how many times has a hard-fought victory been followed by a sense of emptiness? Success can drain all of our energy.

All of these emotional ups and downs are not only a part of communication, they are as vital to your sales success as a smooth tongue or a polished presentation. By learning about your reactions to emotional adversity and unexpected success, you learn how to use these reactions in the future to communicate more effectively. For instance, if you have a sales meeting with a customer and nothing comes of it, you have two choices: You can personalize it as a failure, blaming the other person for being too blind to the value of what you offer, or you can review the experience to learn what you can about what did and didn't work for future reference. Perhaps you became so wrapped up in your presentation that you failed to notice a whole series of nonverbal signals the customer was sending that very clearly said: "I have other important things on my mind and cannot focus my full attention on you today."

Learning to communicate means learning from an experience like this. If, on reflection, you discovered that your customer really was facing an unrelated crisis, you would realize that you could try again, at a time that both of you agree is a better one. The sale would not be lost. If you had chosen to regard the failed meeting as a failure on your part or the customer's fault, you would miss an opportunity. All of this is based on a series of twitches, glances, hurried breaks for phone calls, and so on, which might have told you it was time to reschedule.

In this situation, why wouldn't the customer simply ask you to come back? Because it's human nature to feel that we can still continue to take care of business even when pressing concerns distract us, another communications problem. In this case, the customer may have failed to see what was going on: an internal communications failure with two issues in conflict resulting in inaction on both.

## LISTENING

If I'm making the sales process sound like therapy, to a certain degree it is. That's because, like selling, counseling is a communications process. A good therapist has the ability to focus on the process of communicating with clients so as to keep those clients communicating internally until they reach underlying issues that are causing conflicts. Until clients unearth these issues, you have no hope of finding resolutions for them. It is the same in selling: You learn the communication process so that you can learn from customers what issues or problems they have that you can provide a solution for.

Often this means simply listening. Sometimes it means drawing answers out of a taciturn person. You can't always get the answers you need by direct questioning; you may have to take a circuitous route to establish trust or find common ground before someone opens up.

You will also find that much of the communication that proves most valuable to you as a salesperson is unintentional on the customers' part. They will tell you many things that are important while focusing on other issues. It takes a good, experienced listener to understand that repeated references to comfort may mean a concern about safety, for example.

■ ■ ■

As you read through the chapters in this section, you'll start to gain an understanding of how you can learn these communications skills. I cannot give you the ability to recognize important signals or to spot when you're talking to the wrong person. I can tell you what the indicators are that might tell you these things. Only practice will really let you develop these skills. Communication is both conscious and unconscious— or to put it another way, both intuitive and obvious. Intuition develops out of experience—among other things, out of experience that warns you the obvious conscious statements your customers make may not be the truth. Discerning the difference and developing intuition is a big part of learning to communicate and learning to sell.

# CHAPTER 10

# THE
# PROBLEM-SOLVING
# MODEL

Selling is problem solving. When you clear away everything else, two things remain: The customer has a problem or need that requires fulfillment or resolution, and the seller offers a solution. If the two are compatible and can agree on terms, the sale goes through. What you do for a living—whether you put roofs on houses or advise giant corporations—is the same: You solve problems. The solutions you offer are your product—your inventory, your stock in trade, your service, your ability.

All through the process of selling yourself you must be constantly asking yourself one question: What problems are facing this customer that I can provide powerful and effective solutions for? You qualify your customers to determine the answers to this question;

the more you learn, the more likely they are to buy. If you fail to uncover important aspects of these problems, they become objections and will come back to haunt you at the most unexpected moments.

## PROBLEMS

Problems are hurdles that you and your customer must resolve so a deal can run smoothly forward. A problem is not necessarily a negative thing. Viewed as challenges, problems can be learning opportunities, pauses that force reevaluation of objectives, pointers to new directions, and signals of deeper and more important conflicts. The roofer may resolve an apparently simple problem: The roof leaks and requires replacement. However, there are many roofers, and there is always one who can put a roof on cheaper. The roofer, in order to compete, understands that the job is not just selling roofs. A roofer is also selling reassurance, status, pride of home ownership, alleviation of fear, and a host of other things.

A corporate consultant may have vital knowledge that can turn a major enterprise around, saving jobs and enhancing profits. That consultant may have the ability to do these things, backed by a proven track record that justifies charging astronomic fees. Charts and figures may trumpet continuing success. Yet the consultant may know deep down that prestige value and business trends account for more contracts than genuine, real-world abilities.

The problems you solve may be concrete, measurable, and obvious—like a leaky roof or an ailing company. They may also be emotional, illogical fears and desires. You must always approach your customers expecting to face a combination of both. And, as often as not, the underlying emotional challenges are at least as important to the customer as your more practical wares.

This apparently illogical situation bothers many self-employed people who don't understand why it is not enough to simply demonstrate a product and sit back and take orders. We often wish that we didn't have to dive into the buyer's psyche to discover the hot button that will make someone say, "I'll take it." It seems like a personal intrusion into areas that are none of our business.

## THE SIZZLE AND THE STEAK

The fact is you must sell both the steak and the sizzle. If you don't address both the logical and emotional aspects of the sale, you'll lose a fair share of customers. Recently a new recording studio opened up in my town—in direct competition to my own recording studio. My competitor was a computer engineer with a personal interest in recording, and his advertising focused entirely on the high-tech equipment his studio owned rather than on the needs of the client base. I watched this approach with interest and even (anonymously) went out and had a tour. It has been my experience that few musicians go into a studio based entirely on the gear it features.

During my tour of my competitor's facility, my host rattled off an unending stream of specifications and statistics until my head was spinning (and I actually knew what this stuff meant!). He never once asked what kind of music I did, what my concerns were in choosing a studio, or any of the questions I've learned are vital to a prospective client in that business. To make a long story short, his business soon failed. I picked up some nifty high-tech toys at the auction, and my customers are even happier than before—but they don't know why. His mistake was a fundamental one: He ignored the fact that going into an entry-level recording studio is an extremely stressful decision for a musician who may be spending his or her life savings for a shot at fame. The problems his clients faced were fear, nervousness, and tight budgets, plus the need to get a good performance in a hurry, to feel comfortable, and to cope with the entire gamut of emotional response that is part of being an artist.

## CONVINCING PEOPLE TO BUY

Great salespeople seem to possess an almost demonic ability to convince strangers that they cannot live without the product being sold. This ability comes from experience and a set of antennae developed over years of training and focusing on the problems of their customers. These antennae pick up common signals and send them to the salesperson, telling him that this problem or that solution concerns this customer. By carefully receiving and sifting the constant input that comes in from even the most recalcitrant customer, great salespeople can seem to have arcane powers. The reality is that they take each problem and match it with a solution inherent in their product and return it to the customer solved. Then they ask the customer to accept the solution.

It's not magic—but it does involve acquired skill. The problems you hear from each customer are not unique. Your service or products solve particular problems, and after selling for a while you'll begin to identify what primary problem is motivating each customer. For some, it is always money. For others, it is indecision, fear, desire to win, or other emotional factors. For still others, it will simply be a new roof (or whatever) at a fair price. Once you develop a mental database of the typical problems brought to you by your customers and compare new customers to that database, you'll start to acquire some of that sales magic.

## SOLUTIONS

An important part of this process is identifying the solutions you and your products offer. By having a clear mental inventory of the inherent benefits of using your products and the inherent benefits of working with you, you'll always be able to make a match between your customers' problems and the benefits you can provide.

Because self-employment involves a considerable personal investment on your part in every customer relationship, it's safe to say that you are a primary asset of your business. That's why we start by assessing your own personal qualities and abilities before we look at any products or services you offer. The challenge is to achieve the relative objectivity required to identify your own strengths and weaknesses.

Résumés, portfolios, and various curriculum vitae supposedly serve as personal information resources for potential business deals. Yet it is a curious anomaly of self-employment that potential customers will rarely ask you for proof that you are what you claim to be. Nor will they commonly ask about your education, work history, or anything else except as it directly relates to the problem the customer is facing now. They are not out to hire you; they simply want assistance in the form of solutions.

So how do you convey your personal strengths to a customer? Start by knowing what those strengths are. Think in terms of concrete skills based on experience, practice, and knowledge rather than things you are interested in. Perhaps you have a talent for organization or the ability to inspire creativity in others. Maybe you are doggedly persistent in the most daunting situations and have a total determination to finish things. Perhaps you excel at explaining complex ideas to people with no background in those ideas. On a more physical level, you may have a large accumulated knowledge about making, designing, or repairing things on a hands-on basis.

These skills are not easy to acquire. They are internal and valuable because they can save others time and money over having to learn them themselves. You'll notice that it's useful to think in terms of conceptual, physical, and social skills. By inventorying your abilities in these categories, you avoid limiting yourself to specific content. Although my brother has extensive woodworking skills, he doesn't limit his work to furniture building. He has done project management, sculpture fabrication, prototype construction, and a large variety of projects that apply his ability to conceive, design, and fabricate unusual things.

When you avoid linking your skills to content, you can often find new opportunities in what you do. You'll be more prepared to accept change or take on a job that is outside your experience but related on a process level to what you know. This process-oriented approach means that when a customer tells you about a problem you know you can handle, you can tell her (for example): "While I write for a living, I consider organization and explanation of ideas my real strength. It seems that your training program could use someone who can bring strength in those areas to the table."

## PRODUCTS AS SOLUTIONS

Most of us are selling specific products and services that provide solutions to specific problems. All this soul-searching may seem irrelevant to the owner of a cleaning service, for instance, who quickly thinks, "All my customers really want is a clean office at a good rate with no hassles." And those should be the primary selling points. However, inevitably if I were talking shop with that cleaner, he would tell me about a job he won or lost because of some kind of hidden agenda on the part of a customer. Hidden agendas are precisely what these less obvious skills are for.

Perhaps the hidden agenda is someone's quest for a raise or promotion. Discover this and you can mention that your number one goal is to make that person look as good as the office by providing exceptional service without any noticeable cleaning company presence. You're in and you're out, and he or she can take credit for a clean, secure office environment.

Every product solves these subliminal problems, and there are literally dozens of them in any selling situation. Fortunately, you need to hit only the top two or three psychological barriers along with the normal benefits you stress in your presentation. Often it is your attention to these underlying concerns that will separate you from your competition and get you the sale.

■ ■ ■

So how do you discover these problems? Your customer will tell you during the qualifying step of your sales presentation. You just have to ask the right questions and watch for the answers in unpredictable places. Which leads us to the subject of our next chapter: needs and desires.

# CHAPTER 11

# NEEDS AND DESIRES

What we need and what we want are not always the same thing. We may need a new washing machine but want a hot tub. The salespeople selling either item must be conscious of which problem they're working with and how each affects the other. If you focus your sales presentation on needs while ignoring desires, you're only attacking one half of the problem. That other half will come back to haunt you before you successfully complete the sale.

We buy for a variety of reasons, some practical and some impractical. Shopping to make ourselves feel better is a common example. Sometimes just going out and buying ourselves a gift is a solution to a completely unrelated problem. On the selling end of things, it's your job to uncover both the obvious needs of buyers and the less obvious desires that motivate them on a basic level. If you can define these two parts of the problem facing buyers and resolve them both, the sale gets much easier.

## GETTING BEYOND NEEDS

Defining needs is often the easy part. You can simply ask what someone is looking for, and, if you're lucky, they'll tell you: "I need a new logo for my company," or "I'm looking for a new computer system to replace my outdated one." In both of these examples, you've reached the first step. However, in both cases there is likely to be an underlying desire that caused the customer to take action now to seek a solution. What made them finally decide that a logo or a computer had become a priority? The answer will provide a direction for your sales strategy.

A customer needs a new computer because the old model no longer serves its function adequately. If this is the only consideration and you provide a computer that fulfills the necessary specifications at the right price, then the customer should buy. But, as any computer salesperson knows, these decisions are rarely that simple. The computer buyer has a set of desires involved in the decision, desires that you should try to satisfy. Someone may want to tell friends about his new state-of-the-art purchase, providing increased self-esteem. He might have read about some new gizmo that he must have even if it doesn't really enhance the performance he needs. He may be buying a machine he doesn't even need because he feels a desire to upgrade or modernize. These desires are curiosity, fear of being left behind, and desire to take significant action to improve the quality of life. The third of these desires is an important one to be aware of.

Many of us have a sense of not being in control of our destiny. We live in times of extremely rapid, unpredictable change—there's nothing we can take for granted anymore. We also live in a materialistic society where there is a social cachet to ownership. Very often, you will end up selling your product because the buyer feels the desire to take action to cope with or generate change in his or her life. You and your product should represent a forward movement even if you're selling something extremely mundane. Consumption is an indicator of progress. As a writer, when I purchase another ream of paper for my laser printer, I have a tiny inner feeling of accomplishment because I've written a lot of pages of stuff. I'm making progress.

Your ability as a salesperson to help your customer take action on their own behalf is vital to your success. We all like to feel good about a purchase, and that feeling often stems from the knowledge that we have taken action to improve our lives. Your awareness of this aspect of selling can make the difference between success and failure.

In the rest of this section of *Sales for the Self-Employed,* you'll learn how to discover the needs and desires that will motivate another human to invest in you and what you sell. Those needs and desires are not necessarily inherent in your product. Increased self-esteem or improving a bad day seldom show up as consumer benefits in a product brochure, yet almost anything you sell has the potential to provide solutions to these primal needs.

In the next chapter, we look at the preparation you'll need to do before you make a sales presentation. The chapter will focus on the physical aspects of that presentation, including portfolios, résumés, spec sheets, and so on. However, you must tailor your presentation both to those conscious needs and to the often subconscious desires that motivated the customer to start looking in the first place. Understanding what caused someone to take action toward change is vital to success in the sales process.

For example, if I'm raking leaves in the fall and my rake breaks in half, I have an obvious, immediate need for a new rake. The need is so pressing that no salesperson will need to do any convincing to get me to replace my rake. But perhaps I've been thinking about trying out a gas leaf blower but put off the decision because it seemed so extravagant. Suddenly I'm facing a pressing need brought on by an event (the broken rake) that gives me an opportunity to take action to fulfill a desire (that leaf blower). The experienced garden center salesperson, while showing me the rakes, might casually ask if I've ever tried a power leaf blower. And the query will be likely to lead to a sale that is several times larger than a lowly rake.

## DISCOVERY

It is your job as a salesperson to discover the basic need that started the customer toward the purchase and then go further and find the underlying desire that can clinch the sale. If you use notes to keep on track during a sales presentation, consider adding check boxes for need and desire to those notes. Once you've checked off those boxes and addressed those needs and desires, you will be well on the way to closing the sale. Even if your notes are mental ones, always try to define these two motivations for buying before you start your sales presentation. We get back to this in Chapter 14, with more on the qualifying process.

The easiest way to practice the discovery of underlying needs and desires is to evaluate your own buying habits after you've made a purchase. Even a trip to the grocery store can be enlightening. You'll make *impulse purchases*—that is, you'll buy stuff you didn't know you wanted based on an immediate reaction to stimuli picked up by various senses. You might smell a batch of freshly baked bread and decide that you're hungry for some. This might set off a whole chain of thought about a meal to eat with the bread, guests you might invite over, or a memory of another time when you smelled that bakery smell. These associations, plans, and daydreams may all occur in an instant, on a subconscious level.

Watching your own reactions to a selling situation is valuable because transactions between people are very complex activities. Your customer is going through a constant evaluation process, analyzing, remembering, associating, and making decisions on many levels. And you, as a salesperson, are also doing the same things. The complexity is multiplied when you consider that both of you are reacting to each other and altering your behavior as a result.

Those of you who are musicians or artists may have a clearer understanding of how this improvisational communication can result in progress. Working together on a group creative activity helps you understand how this seemingly unorganized set of impulses and reactions can coalesce in a finished product that has meaning. Our interaction with others always starts out less organized and gradually organizes itself as we get in sync with each other. This synchronization comes about as we begin to understand each other's needs and desires and find ways to match them with our own, eventually resulting in some kind of mutual decision.

■  ■  ■

You don't have to think about these things. However, making a conscious attempt to observe these interactions and learn from them will enhance your listening and communications skills. And, as a result, you'll see your sales presentations become much more effective, and you might even come to view the process itself as the fascinating matter it can be. Discovering the needs and desires that motivate your customers is only the beginning. In the next chapter we look at how to research and plan your presentation so that it directly addresses those needs and desires.

# CHAPTER 12

# PRESENTATION
# RESEARCH AND
# MATERIALS

By now it should be clear that in the sales process, knowledge truly is power. There is nothing worse than trying to sell something you know little about to someone you know nothing about. Yet many self-employed people do just that as they avoid consciously improving their sales ability. Instead, they blunder into a sales situation hoping that their knowledge, ability, or pure moxie will get them through. This isn't just restricted to selling or to self-employed people. Anyone who has interviewed people for a job knows that the average applicant has done nothing to improve his chances of being hired beyond putting together a basic résumé or filling out an application. As a self-employed person, you're selling yourself the same way a successful job applicant must—and that requires preparation.

Before you do any prospecting, before you design a product, pick a name, define a service, or even start in business, you have to get out and do some research. Selling is no exception. The more you know about a prospective customer, the more likely you are to make a sale. This research is one half of the preparation process. The second half is assembling a compelling presentation that succeeds in selling the prospect on your personal and professional abilities. In this chapter, we're going to look at both the research and presentation materials necessary to make your selling successful.

## RESEARCH

"It's nice to see that you've really done your homework."

This statement is one I hear or see in the eyes of my customers when I've done a good job preparing for a sales opportunity. Ironically, it doesn't take much to achieve because so few of your competitors will have done any research. Often a few informed questions about your customer's business or interests are enough to demonstrate that you have at least made an effort to learn something about their work.

Because you cannot possibly become an expert on every customer, you should only seek to have a clear understanding of what they do. This involves becoming what I think of as an *informed beginner.* This means the goal of your presales research is to acquire enough knowledge to ask a few intelligent questions about your customer's business, hobby, needs, or whatever area has motivated them to meet with you. So what is an informed beginner?

For one thing, an informed beginner has an interest that goes beyond casual uninformed conversation. Beginner implies that you would like to know more, possibly making the eventual leap to advanced knowledge. It's not necessary to go far beyond informed beginner unless you will be specializing in the subject at hand. This is because if your customers see you as an inexperienced but willing neophyte, they will usually show an interest in your progress. In a sense, they become mentors—and often a sale may result from their interest. This only works early in your relationship and only if you've gone beyond the basics enough to show an informed interest.

Start your research by learning more about your customer. During the prospecting process, you should have developed a basic demographic profile of this person. Now you must focus in on him or her personally. These are a few questions you might seek answers for before your meeting:

- *Where do they work?* What does their company do and how well are they doing? You can get answers to these questions by reading trade magazines, annual reports, and other published information about their company.
- *What kind of work do they do?* Are they an accountant, a plumber, or a CEO? Once you

know this, you can learn more about the actual things they're concerned with on a skill level by reading books or articles and asking others in the same profession. When I was writing small business marketing plans, I wrote one for an electrician who was specializing in computer network installation. I spent some time learning the lingo of the network business before I walked in to meet him. I didn't pretend to be an expert; I just made it clear that I was willing to learn enough about his business to help explain it to others.

- *What are their passions?* Passions can be anything from family to new business to hang gliding. What distinguishes passions from interests is that a passion is something this person would rather do than anything else. This usually means he'd rather talk about it too. You may learn that Joe Customer would rather golf in Scotland than eat. A little reading about the history of golf could make an excellent icebreaker. The danger is, of course, that you'll get sidetracked by a passion unrelated to the matter at hand. Just digress a bit and then lead back to your reason for being there. Many of the so-called old boy networks that are the source of business contacts are based on shared passions. Your interest may get you in the door.

- *What are your passions?* The things that really flip your switch represent business opportunities if you can find potential customers who share those passions. Shared interests can create bonds that supersede more practical considerations like price. How many times has someone beat out a competitor because he or she shared an interest with the customer?

- *What are the timely interests or concerns of their business?* Read the recent business press for every article published about their company over the last six months. It's easy to do a computer search in your library or on the Internet to find every mention. Drop a few questions about what you've read during your initial meeting and you'll show that you've done your homework.
- *What are their notable accomplishments?* Are they community leaders, award winners, or recognized authorities on something? Try to find out and then congratulate them or briefly discuss their accomplishments. This shouldn't be brown-nosing; it should be as equals and come from a genuine interest.

Research cuts through a lot of the mental gate-keeping that a customer has prepared to filter out salespeople who don't have useful products. Your preparation can get you through the door, past the gatekeepers, and into the area of the attention that is most receptive to your product. However, you must have a real interest in your customer. If you hate or distrust your customers or find them uninteresting, you're in the wrong business. These emotional reactions are not your customers' faults. They are internal and based on your own problems. Get out of that business now and find something you're passionate about. True passion and commitment to what they do and sell is what ultimately makes the most successful salespeople.

## PRESENTATION MATERIALS

As a self-employed business owner, you're unlikely to use expensive ad campaigns or other marketing designed to inform the masses about what you do and why they might wish to pay for it. You have to depend on your personal ability to convey that information. This is how it should be—as a self-employed person, you're ultimately selling your abilities and experience. Presenting those abilities and experience in a way that relates to the customer's own needs and desires is a vital part of that sales process. In Chapter 15, we'll go into the actual presentation process. However, before you step out the door, you will need to prepare that presentation, usually including some physical proof or demonstrations of your abilities.

These presentation materials can be as simple as a fact sheet or as complex as a multimedia demonstration. Preparing them, customizing them for each individual sales presentation, and using them properly are important to the success of your sales efforts.

Any presentation involves assembling examples and case studies, learning about yourself and your products, and learning how to present those materials effectively. In addition, there is a critical aspect of your presentation that many salespeople ignore: Customizing your presentation to the immediate needs and desires of the customer at hand. Here are some key issues to keep in mind for presentations in general, and for some of the kinds of presentations you're most likely to make.

## Assembling Your Materials

All of these presentation materials deal with one basic question: What can you do that I can make profitable use of? This is all customers really want out of any presentation. They don't care about elaborate introductions, blazing seven-color print jobs, orchestral music, or your Eagle Scout status as a teenager. They want to know what relevance it has for them. Staying focused on this key issue is the heart of any successful presentation. It is also the reason why we don't present anything before qualifying customers. Only after learning what they need and want can we tailor our presentation to address those needs.

I've sat in several corporate meetings where a company came in and opened the meeting by unveiling an elaborate multimedia presentation—prepared at great expense—that, with much hoopla, introduced a new product or service. While these extravaganzas sometimes serve to impress or even motivate a group to take an interest, they seldom sell better than a carefully focused proposal. In fact, because it is now relatively easy to put these things together, they have lost a lot of the wow factor that made them interesting a few years ago. Personally I could happily go through life without any more computer-generated slide presentations laden with graphs, dissolves, and pictures of corporate team members.

So how do you stand out from this expensive competition? By focusing on the basics: Core strengths as demonstrated by previous experience, basic and powerful direct and indirect benefits to the customer, and a clear and concise presentation. These three facets are the only things any strong presentation requires.

Their importance became obvious to me when I worked with a small graphic design company many years ago. I went on several sales calls with them and watched as they pulled out a fat portfolio and flipped through it quickly, showing the prospective clients practically everything they'd done over the past few years, whether it was relevant or not. And I watched this tactic backfire as clients were scared away by examples of very expensive brochures or bewildered by thick product catalogs when all they wanted was a simple package design. My solution was to pare the portfolio down to several strong pieces that showcased the design abilities of the firm and then have a brief case study explaining each sample and the problems it solved.

## Case Study Presentations

Case studies are the easiest and most effective way to present the work of most self-employed people because so much of your work is personal and one of a kind. The case study format is simple, and you can apply it to all kinds of presentations. It includes:

- The situation and the problems involved.
- The way you attacked the problem.
- The results—how well the solution worked and changes you made to improve it afterward.

For example:

- *The Problem:* A small natural foods store was losing clients to a large grocery chain that could beat it on a price basis because of enormous buying power.
- *The Solution:* The small store's strongest advantage over its larger rival was in knowledge and personal service. We designed a newsletter for the store to mail monthly to its customer list. The newsletter had a folksy, down-to-earth tone and a community feel, and it was full of answers to the kinds of questions customers commonly asked about natural products.
- *The Results:* Customers loved the newsletter and responded to its personal, friendly feel. The store responded by placing more emphasis on the personal connections between those who use natural products versus the impersonal and less informed volume business of the grocery chain. As a result, store sales increased 15 percent, and the major grocery chain decided to

carry a smaller selection of the competing product line.

The case study approach is useful as long as you emphasize how you learned from the experience and resolved the problem based on that input. Your presentation must have at least three brief case studies of very different situations. These case studies don't have to be on paper; they can be anecdotes you tell as stories accompanying examples of the work or charts showing the results.

Customize your case study presentation by putting together a number of examples that address different kinds of problems. Then you can choose the most relevant examples after you've qualified the customers and learned more about their situations. In some cases, your examples may take the form of stories you relate without physical support materials like charts or printed materials. It still works the same way. You can keep a mental inventory of these stories and tell them where they best fit in your presentation.

## Portfolios

The title of this book could very well have been *Portfolio Selling*—for the self-employed, your portfolio is your stock in trade, the primary thing you have to offer. Yet unless you are an artist or in the advertising business, it is unlikely that you have a traditional portfolio. And even if your business demands one, many of the portfolios I've seen fail to convey the essence of value inherent in the person's work.

What is a portfolio? Once it was a large notebook filled with examples and photos of a person's work. While many portfolios still use this format, there is a whole range of new media available to use in constructing a portfolio of your work. Web sites, photo CDs, CD-ROMs, videotapes, audiotapes, and other media all can work well as portfolios, especially with the profusion of computers and media players available. Whatever form your portfolio takes, it should be easy for your prospective customers to access it under normal business conditions.

A portfolio is a visual and kinetic demonstration of your skills and experience. It might consist entirely of text or be a full-blown multimedia project with visuals, sound, and movement. It may contain actual samples, references, endorsements, awards, and any number of other relevant items. The key word is *relevant*. There should be nothing in your portfolio that is not immediately relevant to the sales situation you are in now. If I'm in a sales meeting with a prospective client for my recording studio, I won't show off my business books for woodworkers, even though I'm proud of what I've accomplished with them. I might show examples of my ad writing ability but only because the presence of an experienced copywriter might be a plus for someone doing commercial recording.

The fact that my portfolio may contain several unrelated things is not unusual among self-employed people. Our interests and businesses must change at a faster pace than those of larger, more established businesses. However, just because you are a jack-of-all-trades doesn't mean you should tell everyone about all of them. Your customers are seeking expert, specialized solutions rather than someone to do a little of everything.

This means focusing your portfolio on a core strength, even if it means developing two or more portfolios that address different areas of expertise and using the one that is most relevant to the customer you're dealing with now. Better still, carry this focus even further by customizing your portfolio for each and every presentation.

CUSTOMIZED PORTFOLIOS   The concept of customizing a portfolio is simple: Before going on a sales call, stock your portfolio with examples or case studies likely to appeal to the customer you're meeting with. Pull out all the others. This requires a certain amount of prequalifying to discover what problems the customer is facing that you may have a solution for. If you're going in cold, set up your presentation so you can select the relevant areas to focus on as you qualify the customer. Go to these during your presentation. If customers want to see something else, show it to them but explain that you wanted to focus on the areas most relevant to their needs.

Does this mean that you shouldn't tell them about other products and skills you offer? It depends on the situation. If you offer something they may need but are not aware that you provide, a quick overview of all your services, at the start of your presentation, may serve to inform them. However, it's better to stay focused on the most important issues. If they want to discuss another project, either go to it after your initial sales presentation or schedule another meeting dedicated to it.

Keep your portfolio concise. If possible, try to engage as many senses as possible with the use of quality photography, samples, video or audio, and other tactile items. For example, a caterer's best portfolio item might be an actual meal cooked for a serious prospect. This kind of sampling is very effective—but you shouldn't commit to it until you've thoroughly qualified the prospects and they have made a real personal investment in your business relationship.

Use professionals. If you're not an accomplished copywriter and you need something written, hire a writer. Use competent graphic designers with experience creating sales materials. Quality printing, photography, and other media items are all the products of skilled people like you. If you want someone to buy into the idea of hiring an expert like you, then you should demonstrate your own grasp of the same concept.

Self-employed people often face a stereotype of being semiskilled amateurs because we are on our own. This is especially prevalent among employees of large corporations who view self-employment as a temporary condition between so-called real jobs. The unspoken implication is, "If you're so good, how come you're not working for us?" You can counteract this prejudice by using presentation materials of equal quality to those of your corporate customers—or better.

How can you get this quality on a small budget? You have one big advantage: You can be much more creative and allow your professional helpers more creative leeway than any large company. This is because corporate creative people must go through endless revisions, oversight committees, and legal checks before anyone on the outside can see the results. This process stilts creative approaches even if it results in a safe and approved piece. You, on the other hand, can free up your creative help to do something unusual and eye-catching.

The importance of taking both a high-quality and highly creative approach lies in how your customers perceive your work. The ideal perception is that you would be an interesting person to work with, someone that particular buyer would personally like to buy from.

This does not mean indulging in gimmicks or clever copy, however. Sending out hot pink sales letters may get you attention, but the impression you send may be one that won't help you. The same goes for playing tricks or practical jokes on customers, coming on loud and strong, wearing goofy clothing, or anything else that you may think is hilarious but is likely to bother your customer. Keep your presentation professional.

RÉSUMÉS   Résumés are for job seekers, not independently employed people. If your customer insists on seeing a résumé to consider you for a project, I personally think it is better to offer a basic capabilities piece combined with a letter outlining previous relevant experience. It puts you on a different level from a "temporarily self-employed" job seeker. The only exceptions to this are situations—often government requests for proposals or RFPs—that very specifically require your proposal to be in a certain format. If that is the case, follow their format to a T.

CAPABILITY BROCHURES     Although I believe brochures have limited usefulness for a one-person business because of their inflexibility, a basic capability brochure can serve as a presentation tool in a pinch. A capability brochure is simply a brochure that tells what you can do. It usually consists of a compelling headline, a subhead that fleshes out the promise of the headline, copy that tells your story, a features-benefits comparison, and either case studies or testimonials or both. If this sounds like a good table of contents for a portfolio, you're right.

Because brochures have value as marketing tools, especially for businesses that require large numbers of customers, I'm not telling you to avoid them. If you have one, use it to reinforce your presentation—but don't hand it out until after you've completed the entire sales qualifying and presentation process. In sales, brochures are known as deal killers because they offer an easy out. A customer can take one and leave, promising to "think about it"—and that's the last you see of that customer. Don't let your marketing tools kill your sales.

## Group Presentations

For one-on-one sales I do not believe in extravagant multimedia sales pitches because they interrupt the attention, focus, and flow of the communications between you and the other person. For groups, however, a presentation that all can watch has the opposite effect, unifying their interest and attention and offering you the opportunity to get your message across to everyone. It's important to use visual and audio imagery along with a personal focus so that your presentation is effective with everyone in the group. Slides, tapes, and video work well, but keep them brief—you still need to spend your time tailoring the message to the group's needs.

In any group presentation (and I'll get into group presentations in more detail in Chapter 15), you should still seek to identify the leader and decision makers in the group before you start the presentation. Then you should tailor the focus of that presentation primarily to those decision makers.

## Store and Retail Presentations

What if your entire selling opportunity is one brief contact on the sales floor of a store or in a trade show? How can you use a presentation? The answer lies in effective merchandising and display of the solutions you offer.

If your displays are well done and in the right location, they not only convey a message, they qualify the prospective buyer. It's very likely that people looking at paint charts in the hardware store need paint. Once you've determined that, you can go directly into a presentation with only a bit of additional qualifying, asking what they're painting and using the various store displays as presentation tools.

## Product Demonstrations

We've all heard of the famous Kirby vacuum cleaner home demonstration where the salesperson dumps a pile of dirt on the homeowner's carpet and shows how the product works in the real world. These canned presentations have sold a lot of vacuum cleaners. Product demonstration is a critical skill in selling any physically demonstrable product, especially if the customer can try it out too. If you're going this route, make sure your product will perform flawlessly under the worst possible conditions. Even the smallest glitch will kill the sale on the spot.

The various home shopping channels on cable TV are profitable testimonials to the power of product demonstrations, as are those ubiquitous infomercials that have been drowning us in recent years. Watch and learn if you sell consumer products because these demonstrations have been tested and refined to high (or low) art. The best product demo involves the customers on many levels and instills a strong desire to have the product so they can try it out for themselves.

■  ■  ■

Preparing, researching, and assembling the necessary supporting tools before you enter into the sales process is important. The key actions you must take are to focus on the strongest benefits of what you do and show these off in the light of your individual customer's needs and desires. Keep things simple and powerful by using a limited number of examples, citing case studies, and tailoring your portfolio presentation to what you've learned from your customer.

Now that we've looked at prospecting and both mental and real-world preparation for selling, it's time to get into the actual series of actions that leads up to every sale. The first, meet and greet, is one of the most important because you seldom get a chance to make a second first impression.

# CHAPTER 13

# MEET AND
# GREET

"Meet and greet" is a catchy phrase for a very important event: Meeting your prospective customer face to face for the first time to start off the selling process. While you may have met this person at another time, this time you're there to try and convince him or her to invest in you. This is a very different level of interaction from a social or casual networking event. You both have your own reasons for being there, your own goals you'd like to fulfill, and your own reservations about what will come.

Making decisions, particularly decisions involving trust and money, can be a stressful experience for many people. Putting a certain problem, need, or desire that is yours into the hands of a stranger is also stressful. Will they treat your problem as an important concern?

Will you like the results? Can you trust him or her? How much will this cost in money, time, and stress? What if this person is a jerk? What if I make a fool of myself?

These questions are what make the first step of the sales process such a potentially charged affair. Your goal in meeting and greeting new customers is to make them feel comfortable and confident about both you and the decisions they may have to make. Because these people are unlikely to know anything about you, everything they take in during their first impression has a powerful message. They are literally building an image of you in their minds, and this image, whether true or false, is the one that will be around until you change it.

Think about your first impression of various people who are now important in your life. Your future spouse, work partners, friends, people you hire for various things, neighbors, and so on. In many cases, your first impression may have been wrong and has changed as you got to know the person better. This is because many of us don't act like our normal selves when we first meet someone. We often have a facade we erect that gives us time to assess this new person before revealing our true selves. After time builds trust, we relax and let the other person become familiar with the real person.

But what if your contact with someone is momentary or only casual? The first impression is all you have to go on, and that is the impression that sticks. If they are very reserved when you meet, you see them as private and reserved. If they act like mindless idiots through some kind of nervous overcompensation, they will remain mindless idiots forever in your mind.

In your role as a salesperson selling your own work, you have to develop a consciousness of how people perceive you during a first encounter—and then strive to make that perception a positive one from the start. You probably don't have time to allow your customers to gradually get to know the real you. And you will not have the luxury of time to learn more about them. The sales process covered in this and the next four chapters is an accelerated way of communicating with people you've just met. You'll gather information and offer information about a mutual interest, you'll learn a great deal about their personality on one level, you'll try to reach an accord, and—if all goes well—you'll complete a transaction and get paid for your contribution. And this accelerated process starts when you first make personal contact with your customers.

In Chapter 4, we looked at the initial contact necessary to initiate a sales meeting. Meet and greet is the next step in your one-on-one contact. The customer and you meet, either in person or via a communications medium like the phone or e-mail, to find out whether you can help each other. The entire goal of meet and greet is to convey a favorable impression that allows you both to move comfortably to the next step.

## FIRST IMPRESSIONS

The saying goes that you cannot change a first impression. While this is not true, especially in longer relationships, for a sales meeting it is true because you are trying to complete a transaction during this early part of your relationship. What is a first impression? Let's say I walk into a meeting with a potential client late, unshaven, somewhat disheveled, and having forgotten my briefcase containing all my presentation materials. It's very likely that as soon as my prospect gets a good look at me, he or she adopts one firm goal for our meeting: To get it over with and get this guy out of his or her life as fast as possible. And there is little I can do to change that goal.

Now imagine I show up early, dressed professionally in clothing similar to my client's, have a positive look on my face, act alert, and am carrying an interesting package? Before I've even said a word, my client has decided that he or she can at least look forward to a reasonably professional conversation that may be beneficial. It may even turn out to be an interesting break from routine and a chance to learn something new. The client's expectations and goals are forward looking and positive.

As obvious as this all may seem, an extraordinary number of people do not take care of these basic details before meeting a new customer. There are a number of reasons why. They want to fail and get out as soon as possible because they lack confidence. They have a poor self-image, which they subconsciously reinforce by dressing themselves down. They're completely un-organized and are always playing catch-up with their schedules. Or they are simply not focusing enough conscious attention on what they are doing right now, as they walk into the meeting.

## AIDA

Experts often apply the AIDA formula to all aspects of a marketing campaign. AIDA is a simple process for building desire for a product. It stands for:

Attention
Interest
Desire
Action

Your first impression should positively address each of these areas. The key word is *positively.* You can always get attention by doing or wearing something goofy—but it is unlikely to help unless you're trying to get work as a clown. You can attract interest by being extremely unconventional, but that interest won't last long when the customer soon starts thinking about getting back to the conventional business at hand. You can also build desire in a number of ways that have the potential to backfire or at least get you in trouble. And if you combine all of these crazy tactics, you'll certainly invite action . . . in the form of an invitation to leave the premises.

The best way to put the AIDA acronym to work for you is to consider it personally. You must focus your attention on the matter at hand and do everything you can to make the sale. Your interest in your customers' needs will be what keeps them interested in you. Your desire to succeed is what will keep you focused. And the actions you take can keep the process moving forward. Mnemonic or memory-assisting devices like the AIDA formula serve as a mental checklist you can run over before meeting with a prospect.

## VISUAL IMPRESSIONS

If you are meeting in person or via a visual medium like videoconferencing, your appearance is vital. There is no rule that tells exactly what you should wear to succeed in a sales meeting. In some situations, a business suit is *de rigueur;* in others it is too formal and may put people off. Generally you are best off mirroring the clothing your customer typically wears. If you want to convey a get-down-to-business impression, dress just one step more formally than the customer. If he's wearing a sport coat and black T-shirt, go sport coat and tie.

Visual impressions are much more subtle than a mere assessment of clothing and hair style. Your bearing, grooming, the clarity of your eyes, the speed you move, and the way you make physical contact all have visual components. Making relaxed eye contact, smiling, and being the first to move forward to greet the other are all positive actions. Looking away, slumping, avoiding contact, and holding back all send a message of discomfort. This doesn't mean that you should bound into the room beaming from ear to ear and vigorously shake the hell out of the client's hand. It means that you should take your natural personality and give it a little oomph, the way you do subconsciously when you see someone you really like. Look like you're sincerely interested in meeting your customer, no matter what the outcome. (If you're not, you're either in the wrong business or meeting with the wrong prospects. You should go in expecting to like your customer.)

## KINETIC IMPRESSIONS

For our purposes, kinetics are actions and feelings like warmth, strength, interpersonal dynamics, and so on. Handshakes and other physical contacts convey a kinetic message that most of us are very tuned in to. We immediately sense hesitation, revulsion, confidence, sincerity, and other feelings when we make physical contact. In Western society, particularly in the commercial world, the handshake is the accepted medium of initial physical contact. In some businesses, ethnic or regional backgrounds, and parts of the world, other conventions take precedence. If you do business in a different milieu, you must learn these conventions and have a local insider fill you in on the ramifications of various responses.

Handshakes should never be contests. If someone tries to engage you in a squeezing match, squeeze back firmly and pull out; don't participate. It sets a competitive, aggressive tone that will pervade the whole sales process. On the other hand (no pun intended) a limp handshake conveys a whole range of impressions, justified or not, but the primary negative one is that the party with the dead hand is uncomfortable about making contact. Again, a message may be sent that colors the entire process.

Handshakes and the degree of any additional physical contact are something you should consciously work out so you're comfortable with using them. While a handshake is a universally accepted intrusion into a stranger's personal space, other contacts like arm pats, hugs, and so on may violate those invisible boundaries.

## TONE OF VOICE

Your greeting should be solidly sincere, clear, and relaxed. As ridiculous as it may feel, try rehearsing a little before you meet someone until your greeting feels natural. Have a brief icebreaker in mind just to keep the initial communication moving forward. The obvious subjects like the weather or a news event work because they are neutral and allow you both to get used to the impressions you're receiving. This small talk should not last too long. It's important to get started on the sales process by beginning to qualify. The next chapter gets into the details of qualifying customers, but getting the sales process started is a part of the meet-and-greet stage. As we'll see when we get into the qualifying process, your goal is to get customers to tell you about their needs, desires, and the specific problems they are seeking resolutions for. There is no magic phrase guaranteed to get things started, but it helps to have some options in mind. The most obvious one is a simple "How can I help you?" or, if you're dealing with another business owner, "Tell me a little about your business before we get into details." If you're looking at a specific project like a book, a garden, or a brochure design, try asking what the prospects would like to accomplish or what they'd like to get out of the project.

These openers have differing goals. "How can I help?" is a general let's-get-started-by-telling-me-about-your-needs question. It works well when you haven't done a lot of prequalifying and don't know much about the prospect. That's why so many walk-in businesses use it. Even if you own a walk-in business, you already know a great deal *in general* about your customers because they come to you for a specific solution that you are known for. Your opener only needs to get them to start telling you about their individual situations.

In dealing with another business owner or decision maker, it helps to get a general overview of his or her business and then start zeroing in on the specifics, even if you've done your homework and have an idea of what the business does. Often, you'll find that the owner or manager has a very different perspective on what he or she does. Getting that perspective up front will help you avoid making assumptions too early.

Selling a project is different because the customers usually have defined tasks they need to accomplish, whether it's a kitchen remodel or a software design. Starting out by asking what their goals for the project are will tell you a great deal about their priorities and desires.

The sales process always goes from the general toward the specific and then back to the bigger picture. If this seems confusing, think about any involved project you have participated in. You start with a goal, you break it down into smaller steps, then you get intimately involved in the details. Once you've reached a certain point, you put it back together and have a finished project. Later, looking back on it, you see the whole with a very different perspective because of the experience. It's like assembling an enormous jigsaw puzzle. You start with a picture of the finished puzzle, then get very involved in putting together little bits and pieces until the whole starts to reassemble itself in front of your eyes. The difference between a puzzle and a sales meeting is that the finished product (if things go well) is better than the original.

■ ■ ■

Meet and greet is your opportunity to start things off in a positive and fruitful manner. It lasts only a few minutes but sets the stage for the entire transaction and for future relations with that customer. Take care and focus your full attention on it, and the entire sales process will be a much more satisfying experience for both you and your customer. It leads naturally into the next step—and the next chapter—qualifying your customer.

# CHAPTER 14

# QUALIFYING

Once you've successfully introduced yourself to your customer, it's tempting to start selling immediately. The customer is likely to expect it and may patiently wait for you to start showing your stuff. To do so would be to make a fundamental mistake, however, one that salespeople everywhere make and pay for with a poor closing record.

Selling is problem solving. Jumping right in with a canned solution tells customers two things: That you think you know their problems before they've even told you and that you're not a listener. The message may be subconscious, but it comes across nonetheless and it rankles. You've put your foot in your mouth—or, to use another cliché, you've put the cart before the horse. How can you offer the best solution for your customer's problems if you don't know what that specific customer's problems are?

The answer is that you cannot, no matter how familiar you may feel with the specifications and benefits of your product. That's because that specific customer's needs are not predictable and can cover a great deal of territory no matter how simple your product may be. Those needs are wide-ranging, and the customer may not be aware of them consciously. That's where the qualifying step comes in.

When you qualify a customer, you become a psychologist, a confidant, and a private investigator. These three roles have several things in common: You must listen without preconceived notions, remember that the customer will eventually tell you what you need to know even if he or she doesn't consciously wish to, and respect the confidentiality of what you learn.

There are two reasons for qualifying: The first is to find out whether you're talking to a real customer—someone who is a qualified buyer. The second is to discover each and every problem faced by the customer so that you can include solutions for those problems in your presentation.

## QUALIFIED BUYERS

A qualified buyer is a person who has a problem, need, or desire that you can solve and who has the will and the ability to buy that solution. These are the first things you need to determine about the prospect. Let's look at this critical step in three ways:

■ *Can you help?* If prospects have a problem you can't solve, stop the sales process now. If possible, tell them that you've identified the problem they face and that you are not the person they are looking for. Give them a referral if possible and thank them for their time.

■ *Are you talking to the decision maker?* If the prospect cannot make the actual go-ahead decision to do business with you, you're not dealing with the final person you must sell to. If this is the case, you have a couple of choices. First, you should keep qualifying to find out who the decision maker is or what process the decision must go though. Then you should determine whether the person you're talking to is necessary to the process or a dead end. If the latter, stop and thank him for the time, then go after the right person. If you need this person's help, then your new goal in the presentation is to make him your ally.

■ *Is the prospect willing and able to pay your price?* When I was selling cars, I had to learn the hard way that you don't spend a lot of time pitching luxury cars to people who have no chance of buying them, even if they would love to own them. You must determine their ability to pay and their willingness. These are two separate issues. You may know your customer is a millionaire. That tells you she is capable of paying. You must determine whether she is willing to do so. If not, you can simply abbreviate the process, go right to the close, name your price, and ask if she is interested. It's not pretty, but it will put the truth on the table. Otherwise, wind things up and get out.

The importance of this first part of qualifying is enormous. The answers you get will tell you whether or not to continue. If the customer doesn't qualify on these levels (need, decision-maker status, and ability and willingness to pay), then you are finished. Unfortunately, there is a strong tendency to not want to give up at this stage. You've come so far only to find you're in the wrong place. You're tempted to keep on trying in the hope that you'll be the one who changes things. Don't do it.

One of the secrets of successful sales is to sell only to people who are buyers. Buyers fit these criteria: They need your product, they can make the decision to buy, and they are able and willing to pay. Get away from nonbuyers and focus on qualified buyers, and your closing ratio will rise dramatically.

## Looky-Lous

In the more cynical sales rooms these nonbuyers are known as time wasters and looky-lous—and by many other less polite epithets as well. This negative attitude is a reflection on the salespeople who espouse it. It simply says that they didn't do their jobs and ended up wasting time on someone who wasn't ready or qualified. There is nothing wrong with people exploring a situation as lookers. Maybe their boss sent them to check you out. Maybe they have a project in the pipeline and they're doing some informal research. Maybe it's a rainy day and they had nothing better to do. Whatever the situation, it has nothing inherently bad about it, and they may one day become decision makers with control over the necessary dollars. Rudeness at this stage is simply bad business.

So how do you qualify for active buyer status? Listen for clues indicating that the prospect is going to have to consult someone else. Ask time-frame questions like "When will you be making a decision?" If you emphasize the word *you*, they may correct you and tell you who will be making the choice.

Ask money questions. "How much have you budgeted for this purchase?" or "What price range were you working with?" The person without control is less likely to give you specifics.

What if they tell you they're looking for something close to what you do but not your particular product? You make a judgment on how well your solutions will fit their needs and decide whether to go further. Perhaps you can sell them half of the solution and refer them to someone else for the other half. Many effective partnerships among self-employed people work like this. When I was a freelance ad writer, my customers were always asking about designers, printers, mailing houses, and ad agencies. I had informal relationships with all of these service providers and could act as a resource for these other businesses, providing my client with a measure of one-stop shopping.

Sometimes you will get far into the sales process before you discover that you're working with the wrong person. It will often come out at the closing stage when things suddenly stall. All you can do is try to go through this person to the right one and enlist your first prospect as an ally. If that doesn't work, then you chalk it up to experience and spend a little time analyzing what happened and trying to identify cues you missed.

## Do You Want to Go Further?

There is another qualification issue that is very important to self-employed people. It involves the questions of continuing when you realize there is something about the situation that makes you uncomfortable. Perhaps you have a bad feeling, question the ethics of the process, or simply don't like the person. It is very important to understand and accept that you have the right and ability to say no yourself. You can stop the process at any time, say you're sorry, and bow out.

Saying no to business is a difficult thing to do, especially when you need the money or the work. The ability to say no to marginal customers is a valuable skill both for your business and for your self-esteem. Paradoxically, saying no to a job or a sale always seems to result in something better taking its place. I don't pretend to understand why this happens, but I believe it has something to do with keeping yourself aimed at your goals without compromise. As the saying goes, be careful what you ask for because you just might get it. Set your sights higher, and you will go higher.

## IDENTIFYING THE CORE PROBLEM

The next qualifying challenge is to identify the core problem facing your customer. Core problems are the basic ones that you'll have to deal with before a solution is complete. In any problem-solving event, there is usually a central problem that, when resolved, helps you to take care of all the other issues involved. Core problems typically fit into one of only a few categories. For example, people in the design business say that you need any two of three things: time, money, and ideas. With 95 percent of your customers, these constitute likely candidates for core problems. Let's imagine you own a garden center and a customer wants to purchase a gas-powered weed trimmer. His problem would appear to be rampant weed growth. The solutions to the problem might include hiring a landscaper to whack the weeds, clipping them with an inexpensive hand clipper, or buying the power tool. If he has money but no time, he'll hire the pro. If he has time but no money, he'll buy the cheap clippers and spend his time clipping. Instead, he decides that someone's brilliant idea (a labor-saving weed whacker) jibes with his own resources. He has an idea and enough money and will save time as a result.

The permutations of these three core problems are endless. A customer may hire you for any one, two, or three of these needs. When you seek to discover the core problems faced by your customer, look for indicators of a lack of time, of money, or of ideas. If you find that lack and can help with it, you'll be on the way to a sale. Let's look at ways to spot each core problem.

## Time

Time-related problems are a fact of life in today's world. With two wage earners in most families, just finding time to spend with loved ones is a challenge. Add in pressure to hit deadlines and the inevitable unexpected interruptions, and we are all living in a place where time is a most valuable commodity. The things you can do to save time for your customers are extremely valuable selling points. Before you can use them, however, you must discover how time factors into the decision to buy.

PROJECTS   In a project sale, it's perfectly acceptable to come right out and ask for a time frame. Knowing a deadline is a start, but you must also uncover the reason behind that deadline, the consequences of missing it, and the problems that might cause the customer to miss it. These considerations make dealing with time problems more than simply promising to make a deadline. They tell you a lot about the pressures facing the customers and offer you many opportunities to help them with these pressures in ways they may not have considered.

Your qualification step should have several time-related questions, starting with the time frame question. They are:

- When do you need to finish this project?
- Why is this deadline important?
- What happens if you miss this deadline?
- Are there advantages to beating the deadline?
- What obstacles do you face that could cause you to miss your deadline?

Additional time-related questions address scheduling and resource availability:

- Arc there stages of progress involved, and do they have individual deadlines?
- Can you get the resources you need in time to make each deadline?
- Are you having problems finding any resources? (This question will also help uncover problems with money or decision making.)

PRODUCTS  Project sales are not the only sales that deal with time problems. People buy things and services to save time. In fact, the majority of self-employed businesses exist because of your ability to provide expert products that save enough time and money to justify a purchase. If I am a computer trainer, I'm not just selling my ability to teach a particular software package to a group, I'm selling a much faster implementation or learning curve. People enrolled in my class will be productive faster.

Time questions for products and services seek information about the way the customer has handled the problem previously and about the time cost of doing the tasks that the product or service addresses. They include:

- What have you been using up to now, and how well has it worked for you?
- Why are you considering changing or adding this new product?
- What is your understanding of how our product works? (Pay careful attention here. It is very common for a self-employed person with a very clear conception of his product's strengths to forget that others may have a very different idea of what he does.)

Like all the questions in this chapter, these time-related questions help you gather specific information about what your customer needs. Try to develop a clear picture of the time aspects of the problem so that you can methodically address them later.

## Money

Money and time, in business, are intimately related. When we're on our own time pursuing a hobby or personal interest, these issues take on a different cast.

However, you must still bear in mind that money is a measure of time. Using this concept is a powerful sales tool. Many customers have never considered the real dollars-and-cents cost of wasted or saved time. You could just say that every hour an employee sits around while a computer system is down costs so much in lost productivity, wages, and so on. However, qualifying works best when you allow customers to define the scope of their problems for themselves.

You can do this by asking questions that force the customer to consider the problem in a new light. This has the effect of demonstrating that you are an expert based on the questions you ask. In the process, customers often sell themselves on their need to solve the problem now. Effective qualifying can make the sale by itself.

Money questions come after time because once you know the time implications of the sale, you can begin to put a real value on your product, a value far beyond the price. If you can sell your product as an investment rather than an expense, you'll eliminate many of the price objections that can bog down a sale.

Your questions should build the overall cost of letting the problem or need go unresolved. This adds the element of urgency to the sale. You do this by asking questions that cause the customer to start mentally adding up the cost of procrastination. These include:

- How much time have you lost because of the problem you face?

- How much does this time cost in actual salaries and overhead?
- How much are you losing in productivity?

As intrusive as these questions may seem, you must ask them to help customers establish a price tag for living with the problem, a price tag that you can beat with your product. Explain that you know that you're delving into confidential areas but that you need the information to help them save money whether they buy from you or not. Treat this inquiry as an exercise in looking at their business.

## Ideas

Your customers are probably immersed in their own worlds. Who is not, after all? This immersion in work, family, and other interests is normal. However, it carries a price—it limits our worldview. None of us are objective in our vision of the world. We see it in terms of our own needs, priorities, and problems. This tunnel vision is one of the primary reasons why we seek people and products to help us with things we do not have time to learn for ourselves. As an expert outside resource for a specific set of solutions, you offer your customers a very precious thing: Perspective. That perspective results in new ways of looking at their problems and new solutions. In other words, ideas.

A new product is the embodiment of a new idea. A new product may have been around for a thousand years but it is still new to the customer who was unaware of it. Ideas are the most precious form of information because they build businesses, solve problems large and small, and expand the lives of those who encounter them at the right time. This "light bulb" effect is a very powerful selling point. Your idea-related qualifying questions give you the opportunity to offer the gift of a powerful and relevant idea to your customer.

Idea-related questions are much more specific to each sales situation than time and money questions because ideas take so many forms—ranging from a new tool to a new market for the customer's business. The questions you ask aim at finding places where you can insert an idea related to your business. It is a little like those subliminal ad techniques that were tried in the sixties—you know, where they flashed a message quickly in the midst of an advertisement or between frames of a movie. You're not seeking to deceive or trick your customer, though—you're leaving a few ideas here and there in the hope that they will act as seeds. These seeds should grow into a desire for your product.

Idea questions are open ended and often involve some improvisation on your part. For instance:

- In a perfect world, what would you like to get out of this meeting (project, product, whatever)?
- If you could find a person who was capable of these things, how would you use them?

- What if you tried this . . . ?
- Do you have any experience with . . . ?

The first question, known as the *perfect world* question, is an excellent opener for the qualifying process because it allows the customer to start discussing his or her needs without restraints. This is so foreign to many people that you may have to gently remind them that they're in a perfect world and are free to fantasize. Typically, they'll give you a complete list of things they want, many of which you may easily provide without ever having to invoke that perfect world again.

The perfect world question, like many of the idea-related questions, has the effect of relaxing the sales process by introducing an almost childlike game to the often stressful decision-making process. This is a point where you must exercise a degree of control, gently steering the conversation back to reality when someone fantasizes too much or prodding a conservative customer to open up and dream a little.

## Self-Esteem

Another core problem that is part of every sales situation is the issue of self-esteem. The customer's reasons for buying and your motivation to sell are both driven by how you feel about the transaction before, during, and after. Because we live in a world where material possessions and net worth are often measurements of success, we tend to directly tie our sense of self-worth to our ability to negotiate and make the right decisions during the process of buying. How the purchase makes us feel is also central to our final decision to go ahead.

While on a philosophical level we may regret that material worth is so important, on a practical level we have to remember that it is. And as a salesperson, you must always watch for signals your customers are sending about how they feel, personally, about what is going on.

We love to buy if the experience is a positive one. Anyone who has bid on anything at an auction knows the satisfaction involved in getting a good deal. Part of that satisfaction comes from the knowledge that you beat someone else's bid. Professional auctioneers recognize and capitalize on this aspect of human nature. The result is that many objects at auctions sell for more than their value as bidders get caught up in the competitive moment. This is directly related to how the participants feel about themselves at that moment.

Your product, project, or service has the potential to affect the life of the buyer in ways you may not anticipate. These effects are a driving force behind the decision to buy. If you identify them and address them during your presentation, you'll be more likely to sell. They represent solutions that are just as important as the specifications, charts, portfolios, and other tools that may seem vital to your sales success.

Experienced salespeople develop an extensive knowledge of human nature because they witness its variety on a daily basis. Greed, vengeance, false humility, pride, jealousy, and other negative traits often drive decision making. Pleasure, charity, desire to please, and the desire to appear savvy are all positive traits that also drive the process—even when they really have little to do with the actual product.

Identifying the underlying self-esteem issues that drive the customer is necessary if you're going to be able to sell the sizzle along with the steak during your presentation. These self-esteem components are what really excite and turn on potential customers. They are the reason we buy sports cars, computers far more powerful than we have a use for, fancy office buildings, and many other products that do no better job than less flashy alternatives.

In cases where the product you offer has a very powerful emotional benefit, couch your sales presentation almost completely in terms that focus on how the product will make the buyer feel. However, you still need to ask the questions and let the customers tell you about their dreams, hopes, successes, and failings. These questions will be answered as you ask the questions we've covered to this point because the answers often lie under the surface. Listen for sentences cast in the first person, for stories of how the person felt during a past experience related to a time or money story. Customers are not only going to tell you what they want, they're eager to tell you. Make that assumption, and you'll hear the answers.

## Listening Skills

You cannot qualify if you don't listen. Only your customers can tell you what they want, especially when they don't consciously know what it is. It's fascinating to hear someone tell you they haven't the slightest interest when their body language, the look in their eyes, and their tone of voice are all saying otherwise. Picking up these signals is a big part of developing effective listening skills. The nonverbal signals you pick up that are positive should be your incentive to keep going even when the customer is literally saying no.

Persistence is valuable—but if your instincts tell you that the person is really uninterested, don't keep going. Again, picking up these signals requires listening skills, and listening means being attentive.

## Attention

Learning to focus your attention exclusively on the subject at hand is a skill valued the world over. The Zen Buddhists have made a meditative art out of attention focused without distraction on the task at hand, however mundane. One technique required to accomplish this attentiveness is to slow or stop your internal dialogue. Internal dialogue is that constant voice that urges you to jump in with comments, that distracts you with other thoughts, and that rattles on during important exchanges. When you're listening to another person and listening to an internal dialogue, much of what both are saying will make no sense.

Practice focusing intently on the communication of others as a preparation for effective sales qualifying. You can do it at lunch, with your family, with someone at a distance, or with a small child. Watch the way they move, gesture, and speak. Listen to how loudly and softly they speak, notice whether they make eye contact, are nervous or relaxed. Pretend you're an artist, filmmaker, or writer who will try to capture the essence of that person later.

Listening intently and sincerely requires your undivided attention. You cannot worry about the future results of the conversation and still make effective use of the qualifying stage. Even if you desperately need the work or money, you must separate yourself from that internal dialogue and become fully engaged in the process that you have started. Nothing else you can do does more to help the sale take place.

■ ■ ■

I've always found qualification the most interesting part of selling. Sitting down with a stranger and learning about his or her passions and concerns serves to move your business forward and enhance your connections with others. Qualifying is also a basic communications skill that is useful in many other situations besides selling. As a learning opportunity, selling is unsurpassed—and listening to people as they tell you about themselves is a vital part of that opportunity. Even more important, qualifying gives you the knowledge you need to make a focused sales presentation—the next step in the sales process.

# Chapter 15

# Presenting

You've made a good first impression, and you've cemented it by sitting down and really listening to your customers. As a result of that listening, you've determined that they need your product, that they are able and willing to make a buying decision, and that they can pay the price you'd like to get. You also have a mental list of the problems that they would like to see resolved if they buy from you. Those problems range from specific real-world things you can fix to the need to feel very good about the purchase they're considering.

At this point, you may well be dying to do a little selling, to make a heartfelt pitch for the value of your product. Or you may be very nervous because it's time to take action on your own behalf. Either way, because you've carefully qualified your customer, you know exactly what to focus on in the next few minutes of your presentation. You'll follow a pattern like the one I'm about to outline, a pattern you will customize to your own situation as experience shows you what works best for you.

This pattern or model is valuable because it gives you something to rehearse and fine-tune. Using a prepared series of steps ensures that you don't skip something important. It also gives you something you can learn more from each time you are in a sales situation. The basic model is simple: You go from the general to the specific. This means starting with a quick overview of what you do and sell followed by a synopsis of how you can help your customers with their specific problems. The final part of the presentation is to present the price. At that point, you will observe a moment of silence—which you must not be the first to break. Let's look at these steps in more detail:

## PRESENTATION STEP ONE:
## YOUR BACKGROUND

This one is simple and will likely be the most canned part of your presentation. You'll start out by letting the customers know that you feel you've got a grasp on their needs and that you'd like to briefly tell them about your business. This overview should consist of a short history that focuses on how you acquired your skills, a quick synopsis of your core strengths, and an introduction to how you will help solve the customer's problem. For example:

*"Well, I think I'm starting to get a good idea of how my abilities might offer you a solution for the challenge involved in this project. Before I get into specifics, let me tell you a little bit about myself and what I feel are the real benefits I have to offer business owners like yourself. I'm primarily a small business marketing expert. You can't go to school to learn small business marketing because they just don't teach the practical things you need to know. I know because I've got a degree in marketing, and I learned more about the subject after graduation than I ever did in school. I've run small businesses and been a part of an ad agency that focused on small business marketing. I've written marketing plans and ad campaigns for all kinds of businesses, large and small. But most important, I think I have a pretty good understanding of what a small business owner like you has to deal with every day.*

*It seems to me that the primary problem you're facing is losing customers to large competitors who are out for market share. You can't beat them on price, so you need to focus attention on your expert services. That means specialization."*

At this point, you still haven't offered specific solutions. And for the person in my example, a marketing consultant who specializes in creating powerful small business marketing plans, this is a danger area. When you're selling expert knowledge, you've got to be careful not to offer too many free goods. It's very possible to give away the store during the sales process—very often, all the customer really needs is one idea that breaks a logjam.

## PRESENTATION STEP TWO:
## YOUR CAPABILITIES

Now is the time to pull out your presentation materials or launch into your presentation. Before you do so, you must mentally customize that presentation to fit what your customers identified as their priorities or core problems during the qualifying stage. This means focusing in on as few as three previous examples or product features that address those immediate concerns.

*"I'd like to show you some examples of how I handled similar situations for clients in the past. I can't show you their marketing plans because they're confidential, but I can give you an idea what they were up against and how it turned out."* (At this point, our hero goes through three case studies, using each to address a specific problem facing the current customer. By maintaining confidentiality, you reassure the customer that the customer's own business will stay private. You also make it possible to use examples that you did on spec or made up if you don't have the necessary experience. However, your hypothetical examples must draw on real situations—and you should disclose that they were studies rather than actual projects.)

*"You made the point that your busy season is coming up and that you'd like to implement these changes before you get into it. That means one of our main focus areas will be com-*

*ing up with solutions that can be implemented fairly quickly without throwing off your schedule.*

*"I understand that your overall budget is limited and that we'll need to be creative about coming up with the most effective places to spend your money, places that will get you the most bang for your buck. Fortunately, there are a lot of options, so I'm confident we can offer you some good ideas.*

*"Although you've never worked with a marketing consultant before, I think you'll find that I'm pretty easy to get along with. I've never believed in trying to come in and change someone's business overnight. You know what you're doing, and I'd rather focus on telling the world about your core strengths rather on than trying to reinvent the wheel."*

In the presentation, the focus was on examples of how marketing plans helped three other small businesses—including specific figures because this customer had shown an interest in measurable financial results. The customer also stressed the time factor, the desire to not change things too much with the busy season approaching, the budget limitations, and a fear of giving control to an outsider. Our consultant addressed all these core problems in the basic presentation.

## PRESENTATION STEP THREE: YOUR SOLUTION AND YOUR PRICE

This is a scary place for many self-employed people. We step up to the plate and go through a quick, agonizing period where we consider what price to charge. Too much and we might lose, too little and we might leave money on the table. My best advice is to choose your price and stick to it. If you must shave it, build in a series of stages as you make your proposal or estimate. You can eliminate some of these stages or features of the project or product to cut the price. Never simply drop your price when faced with a price objection. Let's look back at our example:

*"I recommend that you seriously consider having a formal marketing plan written for your company. It works like this: We'll sit down and identify some specific goals for the plan, as well as a strategy and a budget. We'll also take your schedule into consideration and put in several ways of measuring the results. The plan won't be overly complicated, but it will be specific to your business, stressing your strengths and offering suggestions for fixing your weaker areas.*

*"These plans are typically priced from $1500 to $2500 depending on the scope of the plan and the nature of the business. A company with a large budget and a large market will spend more than a smaller, more specialized company like yours. The price includes two familiarization meetings, the plan itself, and four hours of follow-up consultation. If you're interested, I'll write up a brief proposal and quote and get it to you tomorrow."*

Here you stop and go directly to the next step:

## Presentation Step Four: Shut Up

That's it. You've told them the price (or price range in this example). Now keep your trap shut—the first person to speak will make a concession. Or you'll learn something you missed earlier. Let the customers respond and tell you their concerns.

## QUOTES AND ESTIMATES

Of course, not all sales situations will look like this one. If you're selling a tangible product, the customer may simply ask the price and give you a no or yes on the spot. Services typically require a custom quote like the one in our example. You may have a number in mind right on the spot. Don't come out with it unless you're selling a specific package that you sell regularly or you're selling something very simple. In most cases, you're better off presenting a price range and then putting your price and what it includes in writing.

Putting deals in writing is very important to running a successful business. It involves several things. First, you specify in detail what you are providing. Then you tell, in detail, what the customer will provide you with by way of help and resources. Then you specify outside expenses and who will cover them, a schedule, and payment terms. Finally, you provide a place for the customer to agree in writing, by signing and making an initial payment.

Even if you write up a quote or agreement on the spot, you must cover all the bases. It not only makes you appear more businesslike, it avoids a zillion potential conflicts down the line. Getting a signature and good-faith deposit is also vital because it commits them to the project.

This all overlaps the trial close and closing steps. That's because, if you do a really good job presenting, the deal will close itself. And that should always be the goal. If you have to get a quote out after the presentation, the next steps will take place by phone or in another meeting after the customer has digested the quote and considered it.

## PRESENTING STYLE

It is one of the great advantages of being self-employed that you do not have to become a clone of other salespeople where you work, espousing a sales pitch or style that you are uncomfortable with. You can and should be yourself. However, lack of a consistent message may be one of the disadvantages of being on your own, too. Those slick corporate sales presentations are there for a couple of very good reasons, reasons you may want to use yourself.

First, big companies know the importance of sending a consistent message. They train their salespeople to offer the same solutions and promises that all have agreed upon. This not only ensures that the company can deliver as promised but also allows it to support its sales presentations with other marketing efforts stressing the same message.

You should remain consistent in what you claim, promise, and deliver from customer to customer. Your customers will hear of each other, and quoting a very low or high price to one may backfire later. The same goes for the promises you make and the extras you throw in. I discovered this when I opened my recording studio. A band would come in to tour the facilities and would ask for rates and usually try to negotiate a deal. I soon found out that comparing studio experiences is a common subject for shop talk among musicians and if one band paid less than another, I was in trouble. The solution was to develop a consistent rate structure and stick to it.

The second advantage of a canned, learned-by-memory presentation is that it helps you avoid missing any important points. When Eastman Kodak was selling very large copiers to corporate accounts, its sales force went through extremely rigorous training, a virtual boot camp in which they had to memorize and smoothly perform a very long and complex sales presentation. Because its product had many applications and many powerful features, it was very important to Kodak to have only highly trained people representing its abilities in the marketplace.

In your situation, you probably don't need to memorize a presentation. However, using the same format and notes, if necessary, will make a noticeable difference in your closing ratio. You don't simply mouth a canned spiel in a well-rehearsed presentation—you make a kind of improvisational performance based on a set of basic guidelines. The improvisation comes about as you tailor your presentation to the customer's specific needs, which you uncovered during qualifying.

Be yourself. Just make sure that means being a skilled, confident expert who is comfortable dealing with challenges and enjoys the work at hand. You already are these things or you wouldn't have chosen self-employment. In working with many self-employed people, I've often found that their lack of confidence came from lack of understanding how much they had accomplished just to get to where they are. It takes a lot of skill and ability to become self-employed. Remember that you know what you're doing and act like it when the time comes to help people.

## OBJECTIONS

Because you and your personality are a large part of your stock in trade, I can't recommend learning rote answers or performing a speech you're not comfortable with. Many of the sales training materials available focus on learning a series of typical objections and a series of classic responses to those objections. These often involve turning questions around and handing them back to the customer or avoiding the objection through some clever verbal sleight of hand. These techniques may prove useful, but in general coming down to earth and focusing on the practical and emotional needs of your customer is more effective, particularly for a one-person business.

If you come up against a lot of objections, it usually means you did not do a good job qualifying the customer. The entire purpose of qualifying is to uncover objections. I don't look at them as objections; I see them as problems that require resolution before a sale will go through. The nice thing about problems is that they give you specific things to work with and resolve. If your customer says the price is too high, then you've uncovered an important problem. Your challenge is either to find a way to get the price down or to demonstrate that benefits from the purchase, now and in the future, will outweigh the price. Simply treat a price objection as an interesting problem and try to work it out with the customers. And if you find they are intractable or unrealistic in their expectations, end the sale. They're not qualified.

As your confidence in your abilities grows and you become more familiar with the sales process, you'll begin to enjoy telling people how you can help them. I've always assumed that being self-employed implies a love for what you are doing. This fascination with your work should be contagious. If you find a potential project or sale exciting, tell the customers. Involve them in the process. Let them get their hands on your products whenever possible. Introduce an element of play into the process. Throw them a few freebies—some advice or inside knowledge you've picked up. You'll get the sale and you'll make friends who understand your business, and that means more sales in the future.

■ ■ ■

Presenting is a critical skill. The next step, the trial close, is a test of how well you've done up to this point. It will tell you what you've missed, sometimes meaning that you have to go back to the qualifying process and start over, other times resulting in a closed sale on the spot.

CHAPTER 16

# TRIAL
# CLOSE

Closing means completing the transaction. Trial closing is a test stage where you are seeking to flush out any hidden problems that are keeping the customer from making a decision to buy. You do this by trying a conditional closing of the transaction. Because closing either happens or doesn't, it is not normally conditional. In other words, if you ask people to buy, they will say yes, no, or maybe. The maybe answer is conditional because something else must occur before it becomes a yes.

Trial close is a vital step because it sets the stage for the customer's decision. Many people are very uncomfortable with decision making. They fear making a wrong decision; they may fear losing their money or putting their trust in a stranger. These and the many other fears that accompany decisions make it hard for many of us to say yes (or no). We feel a lot better about a choice when it is an informed one.

Giving your customers the opportunity to make an informed decision is a primary goal of the entire sales process. They must feel that your product will fulfill their needs and solve their problems. If you give them powerful reasons to believe that it will do so, they will buy. On the other hand, if they have doubts or unanswered concerns, they will hesitate. Your trial close uncovers these doubts and unanswered concerns so that you can resolve them.

Another goal of the sales process as outlined in *Sales for the Self-Employed* is to eliminate closing as a difficult aspect of selling. If you master the process and follow each step, leaving none out, you should find that closing is the easiest step. Trial closing is your measurement of how well you have done and your indicator of what you still need to deal with. It gives you a second chance to complete a sale in which you missed something.

Trial closing also gives customers a chance to evaluate their own reactions to what they've learned. This can be a double-edged sword. If they are seeking a way out of the transaction, this step may offer one. However, as you probably realize by now, I don't believe in trying to sell people things they don't want, particularly because most self-employed people don't just sell to one customer once. You are selling a series of transactions in the future. This series includes future business with that customer and with referrals he or she will send you. Make customers uncomfortable with the choice at the beginning, and it may come back to haunt you later.

## CONDITIONAL CLOSING

A conditional close is a request for the sale subject to certain conditions. I've found that you cannot skip this step and go directly to a nonconditional close. Imagine you finish your presentation and immediately say: Do you want to buy this? Again, you've given your customers three ways to answer: yes, no, or maybe. They may say yes—but they're equally likely to say no, leaving you finished without knowing what you missed. In fact, they're more likely to say no in part because of the psychology of being sold. A lot of us get nervous making buying decisions, and good salespeople never give us the opportunity to make a nervous decision because they know we may grab the chance and run.

The simplest trial close goes like this:

*"If we can resolve this, this, and this to your satisfaction, would you like to go ahead?"*

Fill in the blanks with the core problems you've identified and found solutions for. For example:

*"If we can get the plan together before the busy season, identify a strategy you can gradually put in place, and keep the cost under $2000, would you like to go ahead?"*

*"Well, I'm still a little concerned about what I'm actually getting. Can you tell me a little more about what the plan includes?"*

*"Sure, I've got a sample outline right here. Let's take a minute and go over it in more detail. Let me know if you're not clear on anything else as we walk through it."*

The seller tried closing and uncovered a previously hidden problem, the buyer's lack of clarity about the product's features. Equally important, the buyer did not object to the price or the time frame, meaning these core problems had been successfully dealt with in the presentation. Once you have gone over the areas uncovered in the first trial close, always do another trial close:

*"Are there any more questions before we decide on a time frame for getting started?"*

If the buyers say yes, we cycle through again. If they say no, we've closed the deal subject to getting a contract and deposit. If they say "no, but . . . ," you're still in the trial close and you've uncovered another problem.

## Spend Time to Save Time

If the process seems tedious, remember that you're here to solve problems. With many buyers, you'll only need to resolve one problem to get the sale. With others, you need to put a lot of time and attention into their needs before they are comfortable. Be careful to assess your willingness to do so as you go through the process. These time-consuming customers can be very expensive to work with. You may decide to avoid dealing with them. In effect, you have decided that they are not qualified and, while this may have taken time and energy to discover, it's time and energy you will not be committed to providing in the future.

It is very important to listen with all your attention during the trial close step. You are bringing the whole presentation and sale to a head and handing the decision to the customers. What they tell you and don't tell you now is very important. Faced with making an actual commitment or bailing out, people will suddenly reveal important things. You may find out that you're not dealing with the real decision maker after all. Or you'll find out that they don't have the money right now. However, you'll also find out some very positive things. You may find out that they're testing the waters for a bigger project or purchase. Or that they are considering a multiple purchase. It's not unusual to get job offers or requests for you to handle their product as a result of your sales skills. Keep your focus on the immediate situation, make the sale, and worry about these offers later.

■ ■ ■

The value of making a complete sales presentation is obvious when you get to this step. It is a great feeling when a customer answers your trial close by saying:

"No, I don't have any questions. You've done a very complete job and you're making it much easier to make a decision that I feel good about. Let's talk about going ahead." Congratulations, you've closed the deal. But there is a great deal more to closing than getting that go-ahead. In the next chapter we'll look at closing the sale, an event that involves much more than a simple yes.

CHAPTER 17

# THE
# CLOSE

If you have some sales experience, I'm willing to bet that you've jumped ahead to this chapter before even looking at the rest of the book. You may even be reading this in a store, looking for that elusive secret that will make you a "closer." If that is the case, read the book and practice the techniques before you go any further in this chapter. Closing is the result of all your efforts from finding the right prospects to making the right presentation and offering the product they need. It is not magic. It does not require amazing persuasion skills. You do not have to hammer your customers into submission. You simply give them what they want on terms they can live with.

If you went through the trial close stage in the last chapter, then for all intents and purposes you have either made the sale or found out that the customer is not buying. You've eliminated all possible objections by recognizing them as problems requiring solutions and offering those solutions. You've left no stone unturned in your quest to find out what makes your customers tick and why they are there listening to you. And you've been so compelling in your presentation that they cannot figure out how you could know so much about what they need and want. They have said yes.

Closing means just what it sounds like: The transaction must be closed out or completed. This means agreement to exchange value for value. It means that both sides agree what those values are. It sets terms for payment and delivery. And it is in writing or otherwise legally binding on both parties. Finally, it involves actual delivery. You have to meet all of these criteria before you have closed a deal. If you run a retail store, the entire process may take seconds. The catch is that you must do it over and over, day in and day out. Some of you may only need a couple of deals a year to prosper—but those deals may require a lot of time and effort to bring to completion. In both extremes—and in the whole range between—you must still satisfy all these criteria to have successfully closed a transaction.

## AGREE TO BUY

The first step in closing is the one where many salespeople fail, often because they never go for it. To close any sale you must ask the customer to make a buying decision. Read that sentence again, please. *If you don't ask for it, you won't get it.* This is a lesson we should have learned thoroughly as children. Most of us are not mind readers, and we cannot hear your mental wish that we make a decision. And most of us will put off a buying decision unless someone says, "Do you want it?" or words to that effect. If everything is in place, then our decision will crystallize and we will answer that question.

Agreement to exchange value for value is the full description of what closing is all about. You offer something and want something else in exchange. You agree that the transaction is desirable and then negotiate to reach common ground. Start by getting the go-ahead from the customer. There are no magic closing lines, despite all the books, seminars, and tapes to the contrary. If you are seeking the magic words that make people buy, go ahead and learn about all the special closing lines. You may find one that you're comfortable with. That's fine. My guess is that it will be a politer variation of "Do you want to buy this now?"

## Agree on the Value

What is a fair price? There is only one thing that determines price, whether you sell houses or whirligigs: what someone is willing to pay. I can ask $1,000,000 for my house, but if the highest anyone wants to pay is

$100,000, then my price is just plain wrong. On the other side, if I want to pay $50,000 for the same house and there are willing buyers out there who will pay $100,000, then I'm not right as a buyer either. To find the right price for both parties, you must look at the competition and agree on a middle ground.

Big differences in price perception result from sloppy qualifying on your part. If you get all the way to the closing stage only to discover that you want $1000 for your services when the customer was expecting to pay $100, then you missed something, something important. As you qualify and present, you're zeroing in, going from the general to the specific. As you do this, the price begins to enter the process. You may announce up front what you want and then proceed to justify it, or you may build the value before revealing the cost. Either way, your selling should bring you and the customer very close to agreement before you close. If you were as far out as in the example here, then you should have called the deal off long ago.

To close you must agree on a price. A price has several variables. These include what form the compensation will take. It might be cash, credit, trade, or exchange of labor. You must agree on terms. These include payment in advance, payment upon delivery, extension of credit, payment in installments, payment based on performance, or any other agreed-upon terms. Once you've agreed on price and terms, you're one step closer to closing.

## GOOD-FAITH DEPOSIT

For a transaction to close there must be an exchange of value. This takes the form of a good-faith deposit. I recommend never considering a deal complete until you have something valuable in hand. This may be a deposit, a full payment, a purchase order or some other written authorization to go ahead, or an exchange of goods. Whatever it is, your buyer must prove good faith before you deliver.

This is most important on first-time transactions. It is common for businesses to have different terms for first-time customers than for proven customers because of the risk involved in dealing with an unknown. You should be equally careful. Once your relationship is on good terms and both parties are happy, you can decide whether to extend credit, which is exactly what you are doing if you go ahead without a deposit. Get a check signed at the closing stage if you can.

## PUT IT IN WRITING

Unless you're doing a cash transaction, you must get written agreement. It can be as simple as a signed credit card receipt or as complex as a 100-page contract. In both cases, the document should say what is being sold, for how much, and on what terms. And it should be signed by the buyer. While verbal agreements are legal, in many instances they are very hard to prove and do not carry the weight of a signed commitment. As we've seen, even a simple physical act like signing an authorization has the effect of making things happen. You can't go back on your signature in black and white.

## AGREE ON A TIME FRAME

A sale without a schedule for delivery is an open-ended and therefore shaky deal. Set a time frame for completion of the work and payment. This should include a mutually agreed-upon definition of what complete means. It should also spell out who pays for what and what is specifically not included. You can't close a deal that is unclear. Those ambiguous areas will come back to haunt you, and they are quite capable of blowing the deal out of the water.

## DELIVER THE GOODS

Delivery is an aspect of selling that is often skipped over in the excitement of making a deal. After all, you've done the work and made the deal. All you have to do is get the product out, collect your money, and you're done, right? Not if you're smart. Delivery is the start of the future relationship you have with this new customer. It is important enough that I've dedicated a chapter to delivery and a whole section to future sales.

## CLOSERS WANTED

If you read the want ads regularly, you've seen these words in ads for sales staff. The implication is clear: Don't call if you cannot finish the deal. The places that want closers often have an unsavory reputation for demanding that their people sell no matter whether the product is right for the customer or not. This kind of selling involves a whole host of techniques that may pay off in the short run but never work out in the long run—lying, selling inferior products, bait and switch, and other chicanery. It gives sales an undeserved bad rep.

In spite of this, I think you should seek to become a closer for a number of reasons. The closers I admire are a little different from the boiler-room sleazeballs we all know about. A great closer is determined to find the best—the most complete and affordable—solution for his or her customer's needs. Great closers are resourceful in the literal sense of the word, being full of valuable resources and willing to share them freely. They are persistent in the sense that they believe that nearly any problem has a solution and that they can find it. They love and respect what they sell and understand its value on a number of levels.

These closers also have a consuming interest in human nature. They want to know what makes their customers tick. They are sympathetic listeners. They communicate with all the senses and spend a lot of time honing their communication skills. They know when to ask for the sale, and they know what the answer will be before they ask the question. They're not psychic—they're observant. When they find that they don't have the right solution, they always try to help the customers find it, even if it means sending them to a competitor.

Finally, great closers don't waste what they have accomplished. They are not out for one sale; they want all of that customer's business forever. That means responding to the needs of their customers above and beyond the call of duty. They know how much work it takes to close with one new customer, and they'd rather build an ongoing business than reinvent the wheel every time.

■ ■ ■

Closing shouldn't be a mysterious part of the sales process. Often it simply means finishing what you've started. While every close involves an agreement to exchange valuable goods, it is not complete until you've delivered on that agreement. In the next chapter we look at why delivery is so important to your future sales success.

# CHAPTER 18

# DELIVERY

Let's imagine you own a small but exclusive gift shop. A customer comes in looking for a small gift for a co-worker who is leaving town. After a brief discussion (the sales process) she selects a handmade glass paperweight. She brings it to the counter, and, as you ring it up, you realize that it is the least expensive item you carry. Nevertheless, you take the time to wrap it in tissue, place it in a complimentary box, and include a small card for the customer to write a brief message. It goes in a brightly colored bag carrying your discreet logo, and as you hand over the purchase and sales receipt, you also include a business card. As the customer looks at it, you say that you're having a special preholiday sale for regular customers next week. The card is just a reminder should she like to attend.

Congratulations. You've completed a perfect delivery, even though the item was inconsequential and the small extras probably ate up a good share of your profit. What you've succeeded in doing is creating a customer who is very likely to bring in a lot of sales both for her own needs and through the many friends she'll tell about your business.

Now imagine that you've taken an entirely different attitude. You're very busy and as soon as you realize that the customer only wants to spend a few dollars, you disappear, forcing her to search for the perfect item without assistance. When she shows up at the counter, you take the money and shove the item in a plain cheap bag without comment. She leaves—and for some reason you never see her again.

As I've noted elsewhere in *Sales for the Self-Employed,* we don't sell to companies, consumers, market segments, suckers, or rubes, we sell to individual people. As a self-employed person, you only have the time and resources to reach out to a limited number of customers. Each may be vital to your prosperity in ways you cannot predict. That customer buying the paperweight might be the CEO of a company who just happens to be seeking the perfect small gift for corporate giving. Your care in making sure she is happy might earn thousands of dollars in future income. And even if she doesn't pull that kind of weight, she will reflect on her experience and tell others about it.

## NEGATIVE NEWS TRAVELS FAST

If she had a bad experience, she is far more likely to tell people about it than if she had a good experience. In fact, marketing researchers estimate that a dissatisfied customer will tell a dozen people about the bad experience whereas a happy customer will only tell three or four. Can you afford to take the risk of alienating that many potential customers? I doubt it.

## OUR TOWN

In spite of the enormous number of people on the planet today, you work in the equivalent of a very small town. This town's boundaries are not geographic; they depend on what you sell as a self-employed person. Your area of interest, your skills, and the markets you serve are specialized, and the population of people interested in that specialty is relatively narrow. It is narrow because you can only serve a limited number of people well.

The delivery stage of completing a sale is where this small town environment becomes a factor. Delivering a product or service means completing the transaction while laying the groundwork for future business. Your fellow citizens constantly review your performance, both formally and informally. They will do business with you based to a degree on what they hear about how you handled yourself during the sale and afterward. In this chapter, we look at successfully delivering a product, a service, and a project. The key is completion.

## COMPLETED WORK

It is said that half of success lies in showing up—you can't win if you're not in the game. It's tempting to add that the other half lies in finishing what you start—you've got to finish the game to win. The ability to finish things when you said you would, as you promised, and for the price agreed upon is a increasingly rare. If you go into a project or sale planning on pulling more money out of it later or knowing that you can't deliver what you promised, then you have not completed the sale. You're going to fail to deliver a finished product to a satisfied customer.

As in the meet-and-greet stage, you get only one chance to finish on time. As soon as you go beyond what you promised, you are back in the sales process. This is not necessarily a bad thing; there may have been unexpected developments or problems beyond your control. Nevertheless, you are back in the sales loop, negotiating on the very same issues as before. This is not simply a theoretical concept; most contracts go into default if either party doesn't meet time and monetary terms.

Before you even consider selling anything, make sure that to the best of your knowledge you can deliver as promised. If you have problems, immediately open a line of communication and keep your customer up to date. So what is a successful delivery, and how do you predict it? Let's look at three different products and their deliveries.

## Things

In the example at the beginning of this chapter, the item delivered was a simple glass paperweight, a product. Meeting delivery time and cost was not a problem because the product was in stock and the price was on a nifty little tag. The success of the delivery was based on the store owner understanding that she was delivering a degree of service and care above and beyond that expected by the buyer.

When you sell a material product, you must consider physical availability, price (which you can fix at the time of sale), and your ability to deliver it in good working condition. With a paperweight, this is not a problem. If you're selling a custom-built machine weighing several tons and being made in an overseas plant, these become very real issues. Will it arrive on time? Will it perform as promised? Can you get it to the company on time and in one piece? Until you have actually answered these questions by delivering the product, you have not completed the sale.

Failure to deliver has a domino effect, ruining the plans of everyone involved. Successfully completing delivery can make you a hero or at least a reliable resource, both good for future business.

## Services

Selling an ongoing service (as opposed to a project) means that delivery never ends. In fact, delivery is what you do, and as a result your delivery must be impeccable. If you run an office-cleaning service and sell it to a new client, you have committed yourself to delivering what you promised every day, day in and day out. This brings up a potentially dangerous aspect of becoming a little too skilled at selling yourself.

Some self-employed people who have never sold before come to discover that they are pretty good at it. In fact, they're too good. If you're selling readily available material goods like toasters or cars, you're going to do great. If you're selling projects, you can get yourself overbooked easily. If you're selling ongoing services that you personally perform, you're going to get yourself in serious trouble. You won't be able to deliver what you promised, and as you try to please everyone, you'll end up pleasing no one.

Service providers must consider their ability to successfully deliver not once but regularly and only sell until they have a full schedule. Then they have to decide how much selling to do to cope with turnover.

It can be a tightrope act, and it is something many service businesses must learn to excel at or fail.

The upside of this scenario may be that you've discovered a new skill (selling) that is very salable. Good salespeople can write their own tickets in our society, and you may decide that selling is more interesting to you than providing your services. If that's the case, find a good product line and go to town.

## Projects

If you sell projects that have a beginning, middle, and end, you have a very different delivery scenario. You don't deliver until after you've completed the work. In other words, you haven't completed the sale until you have completed the job. Not only that—many project-oriented people are judged by the results of their work over time, and that may mean not knowing how successful you were until months or years later. Because you cannot wait months or years to complete your transaction, you and the customer must agree in advance on what constitutes a completed delivery.

You accomplish this by setting specific goals for the project that are reachable within a certain time frame. As a writer, my goal is to send in a completed manuscript. *(Note to my editor: believe it or not!)* I'll get some compensation in return for getting it in on time. I may receive more if the book performs according to a previously agreed-upon set of parameters.

Leaving a project open-ended is a recipe for disaster because it reduces the likelihood that it will ever be complete. Always build in a delivery date or set of criteria that you can meet to complete the transaction. And remember that you cannot go on to another project with this customer until you've proven you can complete the initial one.

## DEMONSTRATION

When was the last time a salesperson took the time to explain how to operate a product you had just purchased? It has become increasingly rare to have anyone provide any kind of free support after the sale. In fact, we've become accustomed to paying for customer service, warranties, and other after-sale communications. As a self-employed person, you probably cannot afford to offer endless product support for free. However, you can take the time to make sure that your customers understand what they have purchased, whether it is a gizmo, an idea, or a service.

Take a few minutes when you deliver your final product to answer questions, explain features, and ensure that the customer is aware of the potential of the product. All too often I've walked away from a purchase with little or no explanation of the full capabilities of the product. If you design brochures, include some advice on what to do with them. If you sell paperweights, tell the customer a little about the maker or the design that he or she can pass on to the recipient. If you do landscaping, give the homeowner some free advice on plantings or an aspect of the job that you are not handling.

A few minutes spent explaining features and answering commonly asked questions does a great deal to make the sale complete. As a self-employed person, you cannot compete with the mass marketing muscle of large competitors—but you can offer a level of personal service they are incapable of providing. Even a few minutes going over setup or offering free advice on implementation can leave a very positive impression at little or no additional cost to you.

## Wrapping It Up

In the gift shop example, at the start of the chapter, the store owner literally wrapped the gift for the customer. The origin of the phrase "wrapping it up" is obvious, and completing an effective delivery of your product wraps up the sales process. This final polish not only makes for a satisfied customer, it sets the tone for your future relations with that customer, a vital aspect of sales for the self-employed.

■ ■ ■

This wraps up the basic sales process. In the next section of the book, we look at follow-up, some areas of the process we have not yet covered in detail, and the future of selling.

# THE
# SALES LIFE

# CHAPTER 19

# FOLLOW UP
# FOREVER

Selling, for the self-employed person, is a continuous process. This doesn't mean that you must constantly look for new prospects and go through the entire process with them. It means that when you turn a prospect into a customer, you are starting a longer-term relationship than you might think. It is much easier to continue to sell to established customers than it is to start from scratch every time. Building a profitable customer list is what being in business is all about. It takes you out of the struggling start-up stage and into the mature (and profitable) business life. The key to building a successful business is to regularly follow up after the sale with every customer, forever.

Every customer, forever? Why not? Each person you complete a sale with represents a significant investment of time, money, and energy on your part. Yet many businesses fail to keep track of past customers, ignoring the fact that they are the most qualified group you could find anywhere. They are proven buyers who know your product and, if you've done a good job, trust your work. Don't let them slip away.

The first step to effective follow-up is to keep track of customers and keep in touch. This means that you need up-to-date data on them and their interests, private and professional. When you qualify new customers, you have an excellent opportunity to gather data on them. Keep notes on their interests, quirks, co-workers, and any other information as they tell you about their needs. After every sales call or meeting, pull out a card or open your customer file and enter in your notes. This file or card stack is the most valuable asset of your business. Each customer you add may represent years of future sales. Make sure you keep a backup copy in a safe place.

## FOLLOW-UP PLANNING

Because it is so easy to put follow-up activities on the back burner when you get busy, it helps to have a simple plan. The goal of the plan is to make sure that you do not lose touch with any of your hard-won customers. There is nothing complex about it. You simply set aside a few hours every week or two for past customer contact. If it fits into your schedule to spend ten minutes per day or an hour once a week, fine. However you set it up, make it a habit to call a customer or mail a note out on a regular basis.

We're all on the receiving end of this kind of thing all the time. Several of the companies I've purchased software and hardware from over the past year have me in their customer databases because of registration cards I filled out when I purchased their products. I regularly receive updates, tips, newsletters, software upgrades, and information about product seminars in my area. I read this stuff because I own and use the products. I have an investment in them and find their attempts to maintain contact reassuring. They mean my investment is still viable.

Your customers are no different. We all like attention and support even if it's no more than a check-up call every few months or a note in the mail. What's more, these contacts give you numerous opportunities to make additional sales to that customer. They also represent a good place to offer incentives to generate referral business. The subject of incentives in selling is so important that we're going to look at it in detail in Chapter 22.

## FUTURE SALES

It is unlikely that you are selling a product that is a one-time sale—and if you are, you should consider changing your product mix to include reorder-type items or services with potential for expansion. This strategy is one where sales considerations drive your product mix. You leverage your sales efforts by offering additional related products, refills, subscription or dated items, projects that build on previous work, and other products that bring your customers back for more.

You can accomplish this by periodically reminding your customers that you offer additional products that may interest them or that you have added a new service or capability. You can do this through announcements, brochures, direct mail, and other means—but your best bet is a personal call to actually sell them on the benefits of the new product. Fortunately, because you have an established track record, these sales are much easier. You already have rapport—the customer is fully prequalified, and you have a clear understanding of their needs.

## Product Leverage

Developing a product you can easily duplicate or one that requires periodic refills or updates is the secret to really profiting from your business. Your own hands-on work and personal investment of time and energy can only go so far—you are only one person, and your resources are severely limited. There are only so many functional hours in the day, and even if you earn a significant hourly rate, your income hits a ceiling when you use up the amount of time you've got.

In addition to this you must invest a lot of time, energy, and money to develop each customer. To realize the maximum return on that investment you should consider ways you can sell to them over and over again. The answer to the challenge of maximizing your profits from each customer is to sell products that you can easily reproduce for resale. These include intellectual property like reports, books, seminars, tapes, and video. They also include refills, upgrades, maintenance contracts, and other perpetual reorder items.

These follow-up products all have one thing in common: You invest your time and energy in the initial product development and customer sales and then take orders and fill them from a stock you purchase or have manufactured. Each time someone buys one of these products, you are increasing your overall return on that initial investment.

## Spec Project Proposals

Knowing more about your customers' businesses and needs also means being able to create customized products that meet those needs. This is a particularly powerful technique for self-employed people whose work is project oriented. You can approach customers with a profitable proposal for a project for them that you have designed. These spec (speculative) projects involve a risk because you will put work into them with no guarantee that customers will accept them. There are techniques that can make this work well, however—see the next chapter for more info.

## REFERRALS

Referrals are the lifeblood of most self-employed people. In fact, as a marketing consultant I'm always happiest when business owners explain to me that they do not actively market themselves but rely instead on word of mouth. Very few of them realize that word of mouth or referrals are the result of marketing, not a technique unto themselves. You get word of mouth after people hear about you from ads, publicity, other organized marketing efforts, and your customers. All these techniques are effective but none more so than a good referral.

As you establish a relationship with your customer, you should consciously pursue opportunities to get referrals. In some instances you can offer incentives or openly request referrals; in others you must enlist the customer as partner in your success. You turn customers into partners by generating mutual respect and by providing an excellent, high-quality resource they feel good about recommending to others.

The most effective referral-generating technique is also the easiest: *Ask for referrals after every sale and every significant contact you have with each customer.* Before asking, you should make sure your customers are completely satisfied with the work you have completed for them.

If they're happy, tell them that your continued success depends on referrals from satisfied customers and that you'd appreciate it if they would keep you in mind when they run into someone who needs your product. Offer to supply business cards and brochures if they feel comfortable handing them out.

The psychology of referrals is interesting and important to keep in mind. Many of us, when we refer someone to someone else, are not doing it to help that person. We're doing it because it enhances our stature as a valued, resourceful person. Having a powerful reputation for being at the center of things, connected and hooked up, is a socially desirable place for many people. Making referrals confers a sense of power that is very appealing. You should use this knowledge of human nature to generate referrals by never being afraid to ask for them.

Once you get a referral from a past customer, make it a priority. Customers handed to you by others are often prequalified and willing to trust you more than those you find yourself. They are more profitable and more valuable as a result. The catch is that your level of response and service must be impeccable because you not only affect your own reputation, you affect that of the original customer who made the recommendation.

Generally, you'll find that there are core customers who will make numerous referrals. I like to call these my key people—and I treat them like gold. They make these referrals because of a personal interest in the success of your enterprise. You should encourage this interest by sharing successes and asking for input when you face challenges. Sometimes you may even develop a mentor relationship with them, testing ideas and new products with their assistance. This builds an involvement that is good for your business and you.

## THANK YOU

Perhaps the most important follow-up step you can take, whether after an initial sale or a referral, is the thank-you step. This must be more than a mere verbal thanks, although you must never fail to follow up verbally. Thank-yous should be sent by mail and should contain a handwritten note and, if possible, a simple gift. The gift should be something of value, related to your business but not an advertisement. I recommend you keep your eye out for the perfect small gift and when you find it, buy enough to have them at hand to send out.

These gifts should be small but useful or pleasurable to use. Tickets to events, dinners, flowers, pens, quality pocket items like knives or flashlights, and so on all work well. Always enclose your business card and keep the note simple and direct.

This small effort on your part will set you apart from your competition in ways you cannot underestimate. It can mean virtually eliminating competition, reducing price as an objection in future sales, building referrals, and turning your business relationship into one that is more personal and direct. Make sure thank yous have a place in your follow-up regimen.

## TIME AND PAST CUSTOMERS

Many of you will read this and think about customers from months or years past whom you've lost contact with. These customers are not lost—get in touch with them now and treat them as though the passage of time means little. Every self-employed person I know, including me, has customers we've let slip into oblivion. Sometimes you'll run into them somewhere and discover that they assumed you had gone out of business or changed things somehow. Often, all you need to do to revive them as customers and referral sources is to put them back in the loop and start bringing them up to speed on what you are doing.

Start reviving past customers by making a list of them and updating your contact information. This may mean going back to old records, checkbooks, or bank statements and making phone calls to gather information. When you reach people personally during this search, tell them you're doing a mailing to update them on your business and that you'd like to send them the information. Otherwise just get them back into the loop and don't let them get away again.

How far back can you go? All the way, as far as you can remember. In fact, sometimes customers from way back can be very likely prospects because they may be ready for an upgrade or new product to replace the one you originally provided. Or they may have changed sources yet still be interested in checking you out.

■ ■ ■

Following up with both recent and past customers on a regular basis is only common sense—yet many of us fail to do it. With computers in wide use, even the tiniest business has no excuse for not maintaining a customer database and doing regular contact. Most customer contact software is inexpensive, easy to use, and very powerful. The programs all print labels and customize letters, and most of them offer other useful functions for keeping in touch. Fax modems also offer an easy way to get information out. My modem software lets me broadcast faxes to custom lists. I use it to do publicity and for a quick update on new subjects that interest my customers. It's easy, takes little time, and—like any follow-up activity—gets results.

However you follow up, be consistent and do it on a regular basis. Maintaining contact with your valuable customers is a high-leverage, low-cost way to improve sales. Anytime you find yourself in a slump, get out your customer list and start making calls. Call to say hi, call to ask how people are doing, call to tell them about what you're doing. Go through the entire list, leaving no one out—and I guarantee you'll give your business a new start.

# CHAPTER 20

# PROPOSAL
# SELLING

It is very common for customers to ask self-employed people to supply a proposal, estimate, or quote after the presentation or trial close stages of the sales process. Unlike a quick request for a brochure, a request for proposal (RFP) is not usually a brush-off. Instead, it indicates that you have advanced to the next stage of a winnowing-out process on the part of the customer. How you assemble and present your proposal or quote can make the difference between success and failure. In this chapter, we'll look at two ways you can use proposals as effective sales tools and ensure that you create effective ones.

I've already mentioned the two uses of proposals from a sales perspective: to respond to a request as part of the sales process, and to design a speculative project proposal aimed at a specific customer. They are two very different animals. We'll start by looking at proposals created at your customers' request.

When your customers reach a point in the sales process where they feel comfortable that you are a legitimate potential resource, they may simply ask for a quote or proposal. This is common in any situation where you must customize your product or service to the specific needs of each customer. If you sell nothing but a single model of one item with no custom features and a fixed price, then you can simply state your price. However, in almost all self-employed businesses, you are providing a custom, specialized product and you have to price it individually according to a customer's needs.

For this kind of customized pricing, I'm going to refer to quotes and estimates interchangeably. Proposals are similar except they tend to go into more detail, often providing a synopsis of what you will do and for how much. The most important thing to keep in mind when writing a quote or proposal is the needs of the customer as identified during the qualifying stage of the sale. Your proposal is an extension of your presentation, and you should pay the same kind of attention to customizing it.

## RFPs

Sometimes a customer will have a formal Request for Proposal or RFP form. These are documents specifying what the proposal must cover including specifications, time frame, expenses, format, and other requirements. RFPs are typically used by governments and large companies putting projects out for bid; you may often be going up against many unknown competitive factors when you complete one. Your presentation and proposal must be as effective as possible to neutralize these unknowns.

First of all, do as complete a sales process as possible before you start your proposal. You are not only uncovering the important details you must address, you may also be getting yourself out of the faceless crowd and starting a relationship that can swing a decision later. Be complete and go as far toward closing as possible. Sometimes an RFP will arrive on your doorstep or show up in a publication or through an online resource. Whenever possible, call the contact name to get all the information possible and to make sure you're on any future contact lists.

Ask for the proposal package and try to get any other information you can. This includes doing the same kind of basic research you'd do on any other customer. In preparing the proposal, follow the requirements exactly, particularly if you're dealing with the government or a nonprofit organization with outside funding. Often, these agencies and companies have gatekeepers who automatically reject any proposal that doesn't fit their exact requirements. Stick with the format; you'll get your chance to be creative in other places.

If you anticipate doing business with similar organizations in the future, try to find out who sends out their RFPs and make sure they have you in their files under as many relevant categories as possible. If dealing with governments is a primary market for you (and the U.S. government is the single biggest user of consultants and other services in the world), then you will want to include several complete, color glossy capabilities brochures the same size as a letter file. If you don't provide such brochures, your name won't be in the file when the agency prepares its next list of potential sources. And you must update your brochures regularly—every agency has someone with the regular job of discarding them after a set amount of time. Fortunately today's high-quality color laser printers let you have a limited run of these brochures printed rather than shelling out for hundreds or thousands more than you need. You'll still be making a significant investment in the production of the brochure. To some degree this may be offset by the amount of business it generates.

Nongovernment entities may not require such fancy dressing for your business, especially if they are in the for-profit sector, which has slightly more realistic requirements than many of the almost surrealistic machinations of the bureaucrats. Even so, remember that you're dealing with big company systems that are often equally arcane. The only way to cut through these formalized procedures is to follow them while simultaneously seeking to make personal contacts who can route procedures ahead for you. Seek out these contacts the same way you'd seek out and qualify any other prospects for your sales. Once you find them, sell yourself and ask for help.

## PROJECT PROPOSALS

Service and project-oriented businesses write proposals and quotes all the time. You should be seeking to make yours as complete and effective as possible. The general rule is to follow the who, what, why, where, when, and how model. After writing a draft of your proposal, check to verify that you have clearly answered each of these vital concerns. Proposal formats vary according to the business, but most include a brief overview telling what you propose, an identification of the problems to be resolved, a plan for resolving those problems, a list of required resources, a time frame, and a price quote including taxes, expenses, and any other costs. It should also include terms for payment or financing and penalties for late payments.

You can do a basic price proposal on a standard form of the type you can find at stationery stores or in various financial software packages. Most have standard boilerplate covering terms, with blanks to fill in details. For more complex projects, you'll want to type up your own complete proposal.

Send a personal sales letter along with the proposal, and include any necessary supporting materials such as references, work samples, brochures, product info, and so on. Put the whole package in a high-quality folder, stick your nicely printed mailing label on it with the recipient's name, and either hand deliver it or use an overnight courier. Overnight delivered packages get faster attention than ones that arrive by mail. They also indicate that you put a priority on the project.

## TIMING

My brother owns a kitchen design business that requires him to provide complex quotes on a regular basis. He has discovered that the most effective sales tool he has is the ability to get a quote back quickly, preferably in 24 hours. This sets him apart from his competitors, who often wait several days or weeks before responding. The speed of the response also seems to lessen the impact of any significant price differences because a primary consideration in any remodeling project, especially kitchens, is the amount of time it will take.

You should aim to turn around quotes as quickly as possible. We live in an era of instant gratification where many of us can put our hands on an enormous amount of information almost instantaneously. Also, after you've done your presentation, it is important to strike while your compelling pitch is still fresh in your customer's mind. Get it out quickly and you'll be ahead of the pack.

## PROPOSAL FOLLOW-UP

By now you know that I'm a little obsessed with follow-up. This is a very important place to make sure that your customers received your package and found that it fulfilled their requirements. Call after sending it out and say you're just checking to make sure they received it. If they say yes, ask if they've had a chance to look it over and if they need anything else. If they are all set, you may ask when they'll be making the decision. Don't press if they indicate it's still early. If they don't have the proposal, offer to send another right away.

This call probably gets your proposal pulled out of the pile and into the attention window of the customer. It also shows that the work is important to you. Be professional and don't sound needy even if you are. Stay cool and ask how you can help. If they have what they need, thank them and hang up.

You can and should follow up if you don't hear anything for a while. Often projects that were urgent lose momentum. Your call may put it back on the hot list and get you the work. Pace your contacts carefully and don't bug people. Keep the call brief and functional.

## PROMISES, PROMISES

Don't propose what you can't deliver. Ignoring this simple rule has been the downfall of many small businesses. Don't price your work so low that you can't make money. Most proposals become binding contracts when agreed to by both parties—and an overly cheap contract becomes a burdensome losing proposition for both parties. Don't agree to unrealistic time frames or schedules. When you fail to meet them, you lose credibility—and customers.

People usually write unrealistic proposals because of fear of being too high priced, reluctance to admit inability to do something, or hope of later renegotiation—after both parties are in up to their necks. This "planning on renegotiating" strategy can look like a form of blackmail to your customers when you stop in the middle of a project to change the terms. Not only can you be in breach of contract, you'll also cause bad blood and it will come back to haunt you.

Finally, don't commit yourself to too much work. This can be difficult when you're doing lots of quotes but not hearing from anyone. Each quote you write is a promise to perform, and if you write a lot of them, you run the risk of being too successful, a situation I've found myself in and one I cannot recommend. It is a balancing act to avoid overcommitting yourself while staying busy. Unfortunately it is often those times when things are slow that you get the most proposals out and run the risk of ending up at the opposite extreme with too much work and too little time.

## SPECULATIVE PROPOSAL SELLING

As an entrepreneur you took the chance and went out on your own without the guarantees that a job working for others provides. Creating new ideas or solutions without a specific request from a customer is very similar to starting a business of your own. You conceive an idea, develop it, and present it to others for implementation, financing, and assistance. It is the creation of work out of whole cloth.

While such a speculative project may seem far too risky at first glance, many businesses have prospered with this maneuver. Nearly every book, record, movie, and TV show, and many new products, started out as speculative project proposals. Someone came up with an idea and sold it to the right company or person who could move it along and generate profits from it. This concept of sharing the idea and its development and sale spreads out the risk and investment required to see it through.

For example, a book like this one may start as an idea briefly outlined in a letter or query to an editor, who decides whether to look into it further. If they do, they request a proposal going into much more detail. Based on the proposal, they may make an offer to purchase or license the concept as a product for them to sell. I could write and publish the book myself, but that would require expertise and resources far beyond those available to me.

Besides developing specific products for others to manufacture and market, you may propose services based on a need you've identified. An enterprising young painting company might go out and write estimates for painting houses they have seen that need paint jobs, then present those estimates to the owners, jumping past the selling process to the trial close. They would have identified qualified prospects and prepared a presentation or quote for them. Their risk would be the time they spent doing the proposal. If they have the time, they might as well spend it generating new business at little cost.

Speculative proposal selling can generate work when things are slow, as in the previous example, or it can put you in touch with sources of work you especially want to do. Perhaps you've decided you always wanted to work with a particular person on a project but didn't have the contacts required to arrange a meeting. Developing and proposing a project can get many people's attention, particularly if they are entrepreneurial thinkers. This approach is common with artists, start-up businesses seeking angels or venture capital, or self-employed people seeking a first experience to get started.

The most important thing about a spec proposal is that it must contain a valuable and well-thought-out idea. It must be complete on a practical level, which means doing your homework and sticking to practical, down-to-earth considerations like time and money. While there are many books available on proposal writing, I think the best guides are those that teach you how to write start-up business plans, even if you're proposing a work of art or a product.

Business plans are mainly written to generate financing and must appeal to bankers and experienced funders who have usually seen dozens or hundreds of speculative proposals. Because such plans are aimed at extremely jaded readers, they take a very pragmatic approach that is useful for even the wildest endeavor. They have to answer the basic questions—who, what, why, how, and so on—in detail, including realistic monetary and marketing answers. They include the sizzle but focus on the meat of the plan, forcing an evaluation of your dream in the most realistic terms.

## CHANGE-OF-LIFE PROPOSALS

These speculative proposals can have another powerful use, one that can literally mean the realization of your dreams. Just as developing sales skills can make you a better human and communicator, developing salable ideas can mean accomplishing things that once seemed impossible. Many people dream of being movie directors, rock stars, entrepreneurs, world travelers, and many other fantasy occupations. Meanwhile, regular people do these things every day. The difference often lies in how directed you are and how actively you pursue your dreams.

Imagine that you decide to develop a proposal to make that documentary film you've always dreamed of making. Writing a proposal forces you to assemble resources, make budgets, do research, and find people who can make it possible. It forces you to carefully evaluate both your idea and your desire to see it through. Finally, it gives you a workable framework to see it really come to life. It might take you months or years of spare time to finish, and you might need every sales skill in this book to get people to consider it—but once you make that film and travel on that journey, your life will be changed forever.

■ ■ ■

It's my belief that every self-employed person should spend some time on speculative projects—a new idea, a new way of working, or a complete change of focus. These projects teach new skills, put you in contact with new people, enhance your reputation, and inject new energy into your business. Try putting something that interests you in writing and showing it to someone who can help move it along. Use your sales skills to present your project. You'll be amazed at how even a little project takes on a life of its own and carries you along for the ride.

# CHAPTER 21

# MOTIVATION

To succeed in sales you must want to succeed. Your desire to make the sale, get the work, sign the contract, and close the deal is the motivating power that keeps you going. Finding the motivation to keep going until the process is complete and then to continue on to the next prospect is the key to making your business work. Experts in the field often say that persistence is the number one requirement for a great salesperson— the persistence to keep going and see things through until the end.

You probably can't simply tell yourself to be persistent. You need to develop an inner conviction that drives you to complete what you start, even if completion doesn't necessarily mean success. This drive to finish things is one of the primary skills that sets self-employed people apart from their nine-to-five counterparts and one of the primary motivations for becoming self-employed in the first place.

## FROM BEGINNING TO END

Most of us have held jobs at one point or another in our lives. When you work for someone else, you seldom have complete, beginning-to-end responsibility for what you do. Someone else makes decisions, makes beginnings, and makes endings. In fact, it is one of the problems faced by people working in the corporate world that they seldom have the satisfaction of personally completing what they start. As members of teams or work groups, their value is in their contribution rather than their ability to take end-to-end responsibility.

In contrast, as a self-employed person, your livelihood depends on your ability to get a job finished, get paid, and move on to the next one. Sometimes this total responsibility comes as a shock to someone used to the support and assistance built into a corporate environment. This assistance is not only material and labor related, it's also psychological. Working in a group with good management means having access to an ongoing source of motivation, encouragement, and reward that many of us do not have working on our own.

Getting and staying motivated becomes a very important aspect of small business success because of the often solitary nature of our work. When you're down or suffer a setback, there may not be anyone else around to bolster your resolve or help you pick up the pieces. When you're out there selling yourself, staying motivated becomes especially difficult as you face rejection, frustration, or lack of interest in what you're offering. Because you're essentially selling your own personal abilities, these roadblocks take on a very personal quality.

## DEVELOPING YOUR OWN MOTIVATIONAL PROCESS

As you probably know by now, I believe that we learn new skills by learning the underlying process before we get too involved in the content. Keeping yourself pysched up about both your work and about selling that work is a skill with an underlying process very much like selling. The difference is that the things that keep you going may be very different from the ones that keep another person in a similar situation motivated. We each have our own motivational processes.

One part of my own process involves reading or learning about people I admire. After much reading and research, I noticed that most successful people—regardless of field—are conscious of what their motivational processes are. When things aren't working out, they use these processes to get themselves back in gear.

What is a motivational process? To put it simply, it is a series of actions you take that gets your mind off your setback and on to the next step. And I mean specific actions: Taking a walk, reading a biography, going rock climbing, listening to a tape. . . . Personally, I don't think that the content of the action is all that important as long as it is positive and active. It is the actual process of taking action on your own behalf that moves you out of your funk and back into a creative state of mind.

Learning about the motivational processes you use now is the first step. Once you've identified a few things you do that get you up and enthusiastic again, you can build on them or consciously enhance them to increase their power. I like to take a quick walk when the ideas run dry or something is troubling me. Knowing this, I began to think about that walk and what there was about it that put things in perspective. One, I could distract myself by looking at the environment and the people in it. Two, I got a little oxygen into my system and stretched my muscles after too long in a meeting or sitting behind the computer. Finally, I let my internal dialogue settle down a bit, which helped me gain perspective and see things in the bigger picture.

These three processes (change of scene, physical activity, and change of perspective) are all essential parts of my own motivational process. The fourth one that I am aware of is learning something new by reading a book, talking to someone very different from myself, watching a video, or taking on a task that is new to me. Understanding these personal motivational tools gives me a model for creating an even more powerful motivation process. Just being able to consciously access this

knowledge and use it when I needed it was an important realization.

What motivates you? Everyone has a different set
of motivations—things or actions that generate excitement and energy. For some it is material rewards like
money, for others it is sense of accomplishment on
immediate tasks, and for others it may be something
more linear like an ongoing sense of personal worth or
value. All are valid motivations as long as you understand the underlying process. If money is your motivation,
that's fine—as long as you simply use that money as one
gauge of your success.

There are innumerable motivational books, tapes,
videos, and seminars available, and I won't attempt to
reproduce their content here. I will take a quick look at
some basic motivational processes and suggest a few
ways you can adapt them to your own personal use.
Most of us don't really need an endless series of new
ways to get ourselves going. We really need a few steps
that we can explore and rely on when we're down,
bored, or unmotivated. Building and developing an
appreciation for what flips your switch is valuable self-
knowledge. And it is something you can develop and
use as a lifelong skill no matter what your business is
now or in the future.

## Knowledge

It is said that we live in an information-based economy,
one that places its highest value on facts. I think we're
more likely in a knowledge-based economy based both

on facts and on our ability or skill at interpreting and using them. Knowledge is a combination of information, experience, and the skills you've developed to use that information and experience. Increasing your knowledge is an excellent way to reawaken interest in a subject or break a creative logjam.

As a motivational tool, consciously expanding your knowledge of a subject is hard to beat. No matter how skilled you are at what you do, there is always another higher level of knowledge and skill to achieve. This applies without exception to all disciplines. In Japan, where this kind of higher knowledge is very respected, they bestow the title of National Treasure on individuals based on their mastery of various subjects— the tea ceremony, gardening, pottery, other disciplines important in the culture. These living national monuments have one thing in common: They've elevated their interest, skill, and knowledge of a simple subject to an almost spiritual level.

Whatever you do, there is an aspect of it that has this kind of potential. The complexity of the world and everything in it is far beyond our ability to resolve and define. Exploring the known knowledge of subjects that interest you and applying that information to improve your abilities is a process of unlimited expansion. Experienced gardeners know how little they know about the mysteries of growing and continually seek more knowledge. Computer programmers seek to write tighter and more elegant code in an unending quest to create something that works extremely well. Therapists seek to enhance their knowledge of human nature so they can help more people.

Your business offers you many places to focus your attention and learn new things. Read, talk shop with others, take on projects with unknown outcomes, observe the work of others, and incorporate what you learn into your day-to-day work. You'll find constant motivation, and once-mundane tasks will take on a wholly different complexity and interest. And your customers will not only sense this level of interest, they'll want part of it. As inquisitive creatures, we're attracted to artistry at many levels.

## Physical Well-Being

When you feel lousy, you're not going to work at the top of your abilities and you're not going to convey that sense of interest and enthusiasm for your work that makes selling easy. There is an interesting catch-22 situation that goes along with the connection between physical activity and motivation. When you're unmotivated, depressed, or creatively blocked, your natural response is to curl up into a ball, either literally or figuratively. When we're not working in top form, we lack energy and commitment. The catch-22 is that getting out and physically taking action is exactly what our body and mind require when we're down.

There's nothing metaphysical about this mind-body connection; it's simply common sense. We withdraw from failure, depression, or boredom; and when we do, our systems go into a kind of holding mode. Getting out and taking physical action starts the blood flowing, gets you breathing, and reactivates the brain with some fresh energy. You'll notice I stress physical action over activity or exercise. Actions lead to more action. If I recommend exercise, it sounds like work, and work is what got you down in the first place.

Physical action is simple: Get out and do something. Take a walk. Go shopping. Ride your bike. Clean the gutters. And don't just do it once in a while; do it every day. If you have a physically demanding job, find another activity that uses different muscles or allows a gradual wind down. Tai Chi and yoga are both good physical breaks for people who work hard with their bodies, as is stretching and any other low-stress action.

Those of us who are sedentary should add a regular action that is more physical. The idea is to initiate a change in the way you feel. If you're stiff from sitting, do something vigorous enough to break into a light sweat. Pull weeds for 45 minutes. Clean the bathroom. Work out or take a swim.

There is a mental component to physical action as a motivator. By taking on an action that requires some attention but not a great deal of conscious concentration, you free up your subconscious to relax and sift through the problems that are blocking you. This loosening up often yields interesting insights and problem resolutions as seemingly insurmountable logjams break up and the first step of a problem-solving process becomes clear. Work at your chosen physical action and let it happen.

## Meditation or Internal Quiet

As Westerners, we are not taught meditative techniques as children. Or if we are, they are usually attached to a religious or moral dogma that attaches guilt or reward to the meditative activity. Meditation in itself is not a spiritual activity. It is a clearing period and a rest for mental functions, a method of quieting internal dialogue and letting us view the world without comment for a moment.

The power of internal quiet is that it allows many small issues, questions, and difficulties to settle like dust, clearing the air and giving us the opportunity to regain perspective. Achieving this quiet state takes some practice, but it is not difficult. We're not talking about enlightenment here—just a mental respite. That's why in Zen Buddhism, meditation is most often referred to as simply sitting and watching the world go by.

Your own technique for meditation can come from a book or tape, a class or seminar, or from simply choosing to regularly pursue some simple regimen like watching the birds outside your house, listening to the flow of water, or walking quietly. Even in a noisy urban environment you can sit and listen to the myriad sounds around you. Listening to a single sound or watching the passage of light across a room will help you focus and relax.

The primary value of mediation from a sales point of view is that it gives you a central core of calm that remains unruffled as you go through tough negotiations or work with a particularly hard-to-please customer. This center should remind you that a part of you is detached from these proceedings and not dependent on them for your self-esteem or livelihood. And having that calm center will often mean even the most recalcitrant customer eventually calms down and follows your lead.

## Outside Interests

Many self-employed people don't have conventional hobbies or all-consuming outside interests because they've taken those interests and made a full-time career of pursuing them. Our work is our main interest—or should be. However, there is a danger in becoming too involved in one area to the exclusion of other views. Loss of perspective is a major reason for loss of motivation. We get so immersed in our own problems, details, and challenges that we fail to see the bigger picture or even the perspective of our customer.

Taking on outside or personal projects can help us reestablish a bigger picture and often serves to move us forward with our main occupation. Perhaps there is an area related to your work that you've always wanted to know more about but figured it didn't make sense financially to pursue. These kinds of interest areas are good choices for projects you do for yourself, without hope of financial gain. Rather than choosing some wholly unrelated hobby, you branch off from one interest to another, benefiting from accumulated experience and developing a synergy as you acquire skills that work in both areas.

Although I work primarily as a writer and a consultant, I've always played original music. Several years ago, I got involved in music production as a hobby. A music producer plays a very similar role to a film director, helping the artist create a complete work faithful to his or her vision. It involves everything from counseling to getting people into the studio on time and sober. The process fascinated me, but I could see few ways to break in financially and stuck to my writing and consulting.

Instead of making a career of it, I offered my services to several artists and have now produced quite a few projects. Interestingly enough, this creative coaching has been a natural help with my writing and helped me work with small business owners. It also has a direct relevance to selling because in both disciplines, effective communication of ideas and emotions is the key to success.

If you pursue an outside interest, look for connections and lessons that relate to your main business. You'll often find that associations with other people interested in the same thing will lead to business relationships because the trust involved in sharing an interest will work on other projects. It also gives you another perspective on the varying interests of your customers.

## Incentives

Offering and pursuing incentives or targets with rewards is a proven method of sales motivation both for you as a salesperson and the customer as a buyer. Incentives are such powerful motivators that I'm dedicating the next chapter to their use.

■ ■ ■

Sometimes you're just not going to be enthusiastic about a prospective sales encounter. If that's the case, go to the meeting well prepared and go methodically through all the steps of the sales process. The real value of a step-by-step process is that it works over and over again even if you're not 100 percent up. Most of the time, once you get in the swing of things, experience and skills take over and get you through, often with excellent results. In the meantime, learn about your own motivational process and put a little work into it. Try pursuing one aspect of it daily as a reward during work breaks. Remain positive, and your customers will pick up and reflect your mood.

# CHAPTER 22

# INCENTIVES

$E$mployers often offer incentives to professional salespeople to get them charged up and excited about selling. These incentives can be cash, travel, things, or recognition. What they all share is their status as rewards for accomplishing certain goals. These rewards must have a value to the salesperson over and above their dollar value to be effective.

As a self-employed person, you have no sales manager to dangle these enticing carrots in front of you and urge you on to success. However, incentives like these can and should be a part of your own motivational process. In this chapter, we're going to look at how to use incentives or rewards to keep yourself excited about your work. But there is much more to the incentive game than just motivating yourself.

Incentives also motivate customers to make decisions. We've all seen those infomercials on TV where they keep adding more and more "free" extras to the deal to get the buyers excited. You may find that adding a few free or low-cost incentives to your products can mean closing more sales, more quickly.

Incentives are perhaps most valuable to you for a completely different purpose. You can use them to motivate others to act as salespeople for your business. For instance, in my recording studio we sell time by the hour. We have a standing offer, open to anyone who hears about it, of one free hour for each ten booked by any artists they send our way. We offer clear instructions to ensure that these "salespeople" get credit where credit is due. The cost to us is a few hours of free time, which is offset both by the business generated and by the fact that those free users usually end up buying more time to complete their products. At the end of this chapter, we're going to look at how you can build a bird-dog network of your own based on an incentive system—but let's take a closer look at incentives first. (*Bird-dogs* are people who point customers your way for a reward.)

## ENTICING REWARDS

The key to any incentive program is the incentive itself. It must be something that is a powerful enough enticement to motivate someone to take action. The trick is to find what rewards motivate what people. This goes for you, your customers, and your bird-dogs— who are usually former customers.

## Indulgences

Although it might seem that money would be the ultimate incentive, this is not always the case. Often something desirable that the person would like but probably would not buy works well. Call them indulgences. Travel, dinners and entertainment, flowers, and other perishable luxuries work well because once your bird-dog gets a taste of these items, you can offer them over and over. The first time you send a source of referrals out to dinner, you can be reasonably certain he or she will be thinking of ways to refer someone else to you again in exchange for another dinner.

The key to indulgences is that they are luxuries. Luxuries are things you would not normally buy. They are celebratory or may serve to lift spirits or take your mind off something. Sometimes a little luxury promised to yourself as a reward for achieving a goal will serve as an incentive to reach that goal. Offered to others, luxuries not only act as rewards, they make them feel good about themselves, an extremely powerful way to motivate and enlist people.

Besides money and indulgences, recognition is a powerful incentive for many people. That's why sales contests are so effective. The spirit of competition can help many of us exceed our own self-imposed limitations. Recognition can come in many forms ranging from formal awards to informal king-of-the-hill recognition by peers.

## Money

Money is an effective incentive for most of us because we all have uses for it and it is the universal currency of our society. The key to using monetary rewards or goals is to find the smallest amount that will actually serve as an incentive. When I worked as a car salesman (a very interesting occupation), we offered our customers $50 bird-dog fees for referrals that led to sales. When I asked the sales manager why the number was $50 and not $25 or $75, he told me that $50 had proven to be the minimum that would motivate someone to participate in the system—$25 wouldn't do it, and $75 wasn't cost-effective for the dealership. When you use cash as an incentive, you have to find the amount that motivates you or your referral source. (More about bird-dogs coming up.)

The problem with money is that many of us view it as a necessity rather than a luxury. For example, when you give a young couple money as a wedding gift, they are likely to spend it paying off expenses incurred during the wedding. That's fine if that was your intention. If you want them to spend it on something for themselves, you are far better off giving them a gift certificate rather than cash because the gift certificate is earmarked for an indulgence rather than any pressing payment.

The other problem with offering money as an incentive is the connotation that may go with such a payment. An indulgence comes across as an innocent gift, while cash may look like a bribe or some kind of under-the-table payoff. And there are many people who don't need your money and are uncomfortable with an offer of cash. These same people will often respond to a gift without qualms.

## Favors

Favors are very effective incentives. A favor may be a referral back to the customer, help with a task, a trade, or some other exchange of your knowledge for theirs. In my experience, favors are the single most effective incentive when working with other self-employed people, small business owners, and other individuals who understand the value of time and experience. When someone refers work to me, I want to try and do the same for them because I know that a simple referral not only costs me nothing but may have the most value for them. And each time you return a favor, the cycle starts over, creating a referral network that is mutually beneficial.

Favors are gifts of time and experience. Often doing a few well-chosen favors for a new customer may result in a working relationship with that customer. It's very important not to do favors that are the same kind of work that you would charge for. The purpose of helping someone out gratis is to forge a comfortable working relationship based on good will. A good example would be to volunteer to help out a prospect on a charitable or community project he or she is involved with. These projects are often the basis for developing many profitable business connections.

## Using Incentives to Motivate Yourself

You can use all these kinds of incentives to motivate yourself to get out and drum up new business or rejuvenate old business relationships. The things we use to motivate ourselves may be very different from gifts of cash or nights on the town, although these things may work as well. Personal rewards that may work well as part of your motivational process include the promise of time spent on a favorite activity in exchange for time spent selling, an indulgent purchase, or something simple like checking off a weekly sales goal in your planner. Remember those gold stars in grade school? Even a tiny piece of sticky paper often proved a very effective motivator. For many people, checking items off a To Do list is sufficient motivation to get everyday tasks accomplished.

### Finishing Things

Effective self-motivation through incentives means setting some ground rules. First, there must be an actual, specific accomplishment attached to the reward. Second, you must complete the task. Finishing what you start is an essential aspect of the sales process. Reward yourself for completing calls, sales presentations, follow-up, and other sales tasks even if the end result is not a sale. As long as you continue to go through the entire process or step, you've done a good job. And you will close the sales that you want to close.

## Money and Time Incentives

The relationship between your time and money is also an effective incentive. You determine the actual cash value of each action, and it serves to remind you of the value of those actions. Of course, these determinations are approximate, based on the potential value rather than some specific price. For instance, you send out six thank-you cards each month to past customers and people who have done you favors. You keep track of who you send them to, and you also keep track of how much future business or how many referrals come from those people. This is an estimate based on your own experience. The figure need not be exact.

Let's assume that over a six-month period these people generate $3000 worth of business. We'll also assume that about $800 of that is profit that you attribute to your efforts at keeping in touch. You may even know the exact figure as all this income might come from a single customer or referral. If you've sent out 36 thank-you cards during that time period and they resulted in $800 profit, then you can value each act of sending out a card at $22.

Is this $22 a realistic figure? It doesn't really matter as long as it's close. The point is that anytime you want to generate $22 worth of profits, you can sit down and send out a card. If each card really does generate $22, then it is a lot easier to motivate yourself to spend a few hours per month writing and mailing them.

The value of your time in monetary terms can also be an incentive. Knowing you are making a high hourly rate, especially if it increases with efficiency, is a motivating factor with many of us. Even if you've bid a job at $30 per hour, you may actually be making more over the long run because of the potential for referrals and additional sales that may result from your doing a good job for that customer. As we've seen, doing a complete sales job often means much more than simply making one sale. Each new customer's value is much higher from a marketing point of view than the profit on the first piece of business you do together. Consider the value of your time spent selling in these terms, and it becomes an extremely lucrative activity, one that deserves your undivided attention on a regular basis.

## INCENTIVES TO BUY

In the advertising world, everyone knows that the word *free* is still one of the most effective sales words in the language. Offering additional features, services, or accessories for "free" can tip an otherwise hesitant buyer toward a positive buying decision. Look at what you are selling and what you've included with an eye to pulling a feature out to highlight as an extra or add-on. In addition, consider what small but valued items you can throw in to enhance the appeal without taking away materially from the profit.

These items can be simple time-savers like additional free copies, telephone support service, extra consulting time, and so on. They can be future service after the sale like regular maintenance or cleaning. Whatever you decide to offer must be chosen based on what you learn will motivate your customers. If they want free overnight air delivery on a large project, throw it in. It may be the small service that gets you the job over someone who never thought to offer it or added the cost onto a large job.

The time to offer incentives is not at the beginning of the process. Don't put them on the table until after you've qualified buyers and understand more about what motivates them. Then consider which incentive you can offer and add it to your presentation. Consider adding a time restriction to these freebies. This adds a sense of urgency to the deal that may help the buyer decide to close the deal now. Because you are personally handling both the selling and the actual work, you have to be careful about time restrictions. It sounds silly for a self-employed person to say: "We're offering free customer service for six months if you buy this week." The logical retort is "What's different about this week?"

You're better off with something available in limited quantities. For instance: "We've acquired a limited amount of these taped versions of the seminar, which will be given to the first 15 participants to register." Another way to build a time restriction into a freebie is to use things that expire like concert or sporting event tickets. Offering to throw in two seats at next week's football game has an obvious time element involved that may push a decision.

## BIRD-DOG PROGRAMS

A bird-dog program is a system for soliciting referrals from customers or other people in exchange for an incentive or payment. Bird-dog programs are not legal in all forms in some states because of fear that they might involve illegal kickbacks or under-the-table payments for sending work to certain companies. As I mentioned earlier, bird-dogs are a part of the auto sales business and have proven very effective there. Typically a salesperson delivering a car to a buyer will demonstrate its features and make sure the customer is satisfied, then make a bird-dog presentation. Explaining that much of their business comes from referrals, the salespeople give the customer a stack of business cards with the customer's name or initials on the back. They offer to pay the customer a set amount in exchange for each legitimate buyer who shows up with one of the cards.

The key to a bird-dog system is understanding that while few people will respond to the offer, those who do are likely to make continued referrals. One friend of mine liked those $50 checks so much that he referred more than 20 customers over several years, resulting in a significant portion of that salesperson's income.

Your bird-dog system may not involve blatant cash payments, but the consideration should have measurable value. A clear offer of time or products of a predefined value is more effective than a vague promise. As mentioned earlier, my recording studio offers one hour of free time for each ten booked by the new customer. This is a clear offer with a measurable value that has a built-in appeal to my customers, who typically always want more time.

Clearly explain the system after you are sure your customer is satisfied with the sale. You will have to use your judgment as to whether to offer the system to every customer or only to those you consider likely candidates. Personally, I feel you must offer the deal to all your customers. Otherwise, one may hear from another of the offer and be offended, or you may miss out on an opportunity from a customer who turns out to be a great source of referrals.

The ground rules must be clear, and you give the benefit of the doubt to the customer. If some people say they sent the referral to you, even if you're not certain they did, pay up. Once they get a taste of it and like it, they'll send more. If you alienate people, you'll lose both them and their referrals.

■ ■ ■

Incentives are a personal thing. What works for me may be distasteful or meaningless to you. Before you offer incentives to anyone else, make sure you've qualified your prospects and gotten to know what motivates them. Then you can tailor your incentives to fit those needs the same way you tailored your sales presentation to fit their product needs. The incentives you use to motivate yourself are no different. You must learn through experience what keeps you moving toward your goal—whether it's a piece of chocolate cake or a trip to Hawaii.

# CHAPTER 23

# NEGOTIATION

Negotiation is about mutual agreement. It is not about one side or the other winning or taking everything on the table. In a successful negotiation, both parties have received value that satisfies their needs. If you take the shirt off a man's back, he'll never do business with you again. If you treat him fairly, you'll develop a relationship based on trust that can last.

The problem with this idealistic vision is that there are many people out there who only view negotiation as competition or even all-out war. In some cases they are blinded by their desires or by an inflated ego. In others they are so insecure about themselves they can only feel good at other people's expense. Some simply stonewall to avoid making a decision or because they are incapable of making a decision. Some people are just jerks.

Dealing with these people in a negotiation of any kind is frustrating at best and destructive at worst. The only thing you can do is qualify to discover these problems and then decide whether it's worth it to you to continue. In my experience, you are far better off avoiding extremely confrontational negotiations and focusing your energies on those that are win–win situations. If your business involves high-stakes deals—large sums of money, stocks, or other big-time negotiations—it might be acceptable to go for the throat, especially if you don't have to deal with the same person twice. For the average self-employed person, it's not worth it.

Deciding whether to negotiate at all is the first step. Sometimes you may decide to stick to your price and terms and let the sale go if it doesn't work out. With many customers, this is not a bad idea—once you start lowering your price or adding in freebies, they won't stop asking until you're broke. In other cases, customers will peg you as a person who can be gotten on the cheap, a bad impression that is difficult to shake. If you sense this kind of one-sided negotiation coming, stick to your guns.

Most of the time, it's not that simple. Perhaps your product has many features to choose from or many possible degrees of involvement on your part. Perhaps there are time constraints or advantages to one form of payment over another. These things all need negotiation. Price is also negotiable—although I think you should never simply drop a price. Instead, drop features, services, or promises involving time to lower your price.

## INFORMATION AND TIME

Your power in most negotiating situations comes from the amount of time and knowledge or information you have. If you go into a negotiation desperate for a sale, perhaps to stave off a creditor or feed the kids, you'll have little power to make a good deal. You have no time. If you go into a negotiation with a person you know nothing about, you are unlikely to succeed without acquiring information about that person. To negotiate successfully, you must have a measure of both time and information or use one to get the other.

A major aspect of sales is the gathering of information. Only when you have a certain amount of information can you close a transaction. You gather this information every step of the way, from planning to prospecting to qualifying. It requires time to accumulate information of value. Time also gives you room to wait or pull back. You can walk away from a situation and consider it, or you can wait until you've gathered more information.

Power in a negotiating situation means having the ability to say yes or no. The interesting thing about most negotiations is that both parties must share this power equally before a transaction can take place. If one person has the power to make a decision and the other does not, you're going nowhere. However, if you make concessions that empower the other person, they may then be able to decide. It is ironic that negotiation is often seen as confrontational when it is in fact a process of giving things away.

## MAKING AN OFFER

The key to negotiating is the offer. Someone must make one to get things started. If you are a confrontational, winner-take-all negotiator, you won't make an offer because your credo is that the first person to concede anything will lose. So you'll sit there stone-faced and wait for the other person to cave in or walk away. But you have given them something. You've given them only two choices, yes or no, win or lose. And you stand an equal chance of winning (getting the deal your way) or losing (no deal). It's a 50/50 situation.

The person who makes an offer to open a negotiation is telling the other person that he or she wants a deal and wants to work to make it happen. The offer is an offer of information. I tell you I'll give you $1000 for your widget if I can have it today. You reply that you need $1250 and you cannot sell until next week. The offer and counteroffer are on the table, and the two of us are no longer in a yes-no situation. By making an offer, you make the likelihood of a transaction taking place much greater. This is why it is so important to ask for a sale during your closing step. Asking for a sale is a form of offer. You name a price, and they respond.

Negotiating is a process of concession and exchange. We do it every day. If there were no negotiations in our society, you would not be able to buy anything. Even an item with a fixed price is negotiable. If the coffee shop tells me my cappuccino is $2.50, I can always go to a competitor or make it at home. If enough people do the same, the shop will either go out of business or lower its prices. Capitalism as a system lets the consumer negotiate by buying elsewhere from a competitor. In a free and open market, the buyers always determine the prices.

The problem most Westerners have is that we rarely negotiate in person for anything. Unless you're buying a car, a case of fruit at a farmer's market, or a few other things where dickering is traditional, you don't discuss price with anyone face to face. As a result, we're not comfortable with bartering, bargaining, and negotiation. We either accept a price or go elsewhere. As a seller, however, you don't want a yes-no situation; you want to make a deal. So you must make some kind of an offer that gives the buyer options on how to respond.

## EVERYTHING IS NEGOTIABLE

The fact is that everything is negotiable. You just have to ask. Price may be fixed, but other conditions may not be. A pizza costs ten bucks. It says so on the menu. Does that mean you must pay $10? Not necessarily. What if you pick it up? What if you get a different set of toppings (features)? What if you and the guy standing next to you in line split it? What if you tell the owners you'd like their pizza but the guy down the road is charging only $8? Is he willing to split the difference to get your business now?

In each of these cases, compromise is the key. You may give up features (toppings), time (delivery), or your favorite pie—all to save a few bucks. The pizza man gives up money or gains time by having his delivery guy do something else. If you involve a third party, you give up quantity but save money, and so on. Even a mundane action like buying a pizza involves options, and each may be negotiable.

## RISK MANAGEMENT

As a seller, you know what you need for your product: the bottom line price or conditions that will let you stay in business. If you are not aware of these conditions, you should not be out there selling. Part of preparing for a negotiation is planning a risk management strategy. For a self-employed person, this is essential. If you sell what you cannot deliver or agree to an unrealistic price or schedule, you may be risking your reputation and livelihood. Knowing your bottom line is vital because it tells you when to stop and either hold your ground or give up the sale.

Determining these limitations is not always easy, especially if you need the work. It is easy, in the heat of the moment, to agree to a low price or unrealistic schedule because you want the sale. You have to set your limits and stick to them no matter what. If you worked for someone else you might have another dispassionate person approving these things for you. This would give you an outside perspective and keep you from making unprofitable choices. As a self-employed person, you may not have that oversight. Perhaps you can get a friend, business acquaintance, or spouse who knows your business to help you evaluate each situation before you go into a sales negotiation. Set price and delivery or schedule limits and stick to them.

Auctions are a good example of a failure of managed risk on the part of a buyer. Auctions work because people allow themselves to get caught up in the heat of the moment, the competition, and the fast-paced selling. They may have a limit but suddenly find themselves paying too much because emotion took over. Experienced auction-goers know that they must determine their price and stop bidding the moment anybody bids anything over that level.

There is also the risk of leaving money on the table. What if you sold too cheap or gave away too many options? Every self-employed person I know struggles with this uncertainty about pricing. The only way to manage the risk of not charging enough is to choose a number and conditions you can live with and be satisfied if you get them. Then you have to learn from each experience. If the buyer agrees to your terms too quickly, it might mean you're a little low. Or maybe they just don't want to dicker. Good qualifying should help you know which is the case. Then you can adjust accordingly for the future.

■ ■ ■

There are many books available on negotiating. In general, I've found the best are those that treat the process as a mutually beneficial one rather than as a confrontation. When someone walks away from any negotiation feeling like a loser, both parties will lose. We don't "win through intimidation"; we win by helping others while helping ourselves. Sales is not a war; it is a process of communication.

# CHAPTER 24

# INVISIBLE SELLING

The ability to sell yourself is a powerful tool, one that literally changes the course of your business and your life. As with most really powerful tools, the beginner seldom makes full use of it. We start out with those aspects of the selling process that we have an immediate use for and only gradually do we come to understand its full potential. As an organized and focused means of communication, sales affects every contact you make with others—including family members, lovers, and strangers. If you clearly understand the problem-solving model of selling, you'll probably develop a better ability to resolve other conflicts large and small, from disputes with your kids to scheduling a meeting with a group of busy business associates.

The basic process we looked at in Section Two has plenty of potential for most of us; in fact, exploring it as an evolving process can be very interesting in itself. In many circumstances, you may find it valuable to learn more about the subtleties of human communication—by taking a very low-key approach, you can win over skittish or conservative customers. These subtle skills are what make some so-called natural salespeople prosper so effortlessly while others seem to be working with blunt instruments.

Because you are self-employed or considering going out on your own, acquiring these invisible sales skills is particularly valuable. You can do business without appearing to be overtly pitching your product. Often you can go through the entire process without customers noticing that they are listening to a sales pitch and then close with a straightforward request. This apparently relaxed process involves developing a shared rapport that inspires confidence. The customer goes away thinking that you are a sympathetic resource, someone who's easy to deal with.

## RAPPORT

You probably cannot build rapport by assuming a personality that is false. Suddenly becoming an avid sports fan with a similarly minded customer, when in reality you loathe sports, is a deceit that you may get caught in, losing the sale. Rapport is not always a touchy-feely thing, either. One customer may enjoy an almost therapeutic sharing of knowledge while another may recoil from such intimacy and want to stay strictly business.

It is common for most of us to assume that we have an individual and perhaps inborn style of selling. We think it natural that one person may prefer to develop close, personalized relationships with customers while another may prefer to sell via arm's-length transactions. The problem with predetermining your preference is that it goes against the basic premise of all successful marketing: the idea that you must tailor your presentation and product to the needs of the customer rather than to your own agenda. If you only present the cold, hard facts, you'll lose the customers whose concerns are more internal and emotional. If you only make emotionally charged presentations, you'll scare off the pragmatic left-brainers.

Even these distinctions are much too black and white. Every person you deal with has his or her own way of relating to the world, a unique set of practical and emotional needs and interests. Invisible selling means that you must find a way to develop rapport with that viewpoint and use that rapport as a language to make the sale on that person's terms as well as your own. In a sense, you become a kind of intelligent chameleon who adapts consciously to the unconscious needs of the individual customer before you.

I use the word *intelligent* because this changing of color and attitude does not mean giving up your own identity any more than speaking to people in their own language makes you a member of that language group. You remain yourself, conscious of your goals and aware of what you are doing.

The science or art of developing rapport has developed as a conscious process only in recent years. Before then there were many attempts to explain the skills involved, but they always focused on content rather than process. For example, training might have focused on one insight and then suggested that you use it on all your customers. One example might be the "always answer a question with a question" technique. While it would work with someone who always responds to questions, however, this technique won't work with someone who finds questions irritating.

The process of developing rapport involves learning to use a set of communications tools that you can adapt to the person or persons you are working with at the moment. While there are many tools, I'm going to focus on three basic ones that you can explore right now. They have a lot of power, yet you can use them on a very simple level to enhance your communications ability by building rapport with your customers on their terms. These tools are *pacing, representational systems,* and *anchors.* They are based on the work of Richard Bandler, John Grinder, and others. For more information on these techniques, see the Resources section.

## Pacing

Imagine you arrive at a sales appointment on an exceptionally nice fall day. You meet and greet the customer, and he suggests that you take a stroll outside while discussing your business. Your initial reaction is that it will be very difficult to qualify and make your presentation while taking in the fall air—but you realize you have no choice. Your customer takes off his suit jacket, and you head out into an unseasonably warm day.

In this example, the customer is setting the pace. He has changed the environment and the tempo of the meeting. To succeed, you must try and match his pace. If you are able to do so, you'll increase your rapport; if you hesitate or look ill at ease with the change, you'll lose that rapport and the two of you will be in different worlds. Getting into the same world or state of mind as your customer is a good definition of rapport. The first step to achieving rapport is pacing.

So you're walking through a corporate office park on a fall day, enjoying the colors of the leaves and making small talk. Your customer walks at a brisk rate, but every so often he hesitates and then takes a deep breath of the fresh air. You notice that each time he does so, he changes the subject slightly and gets closer to the original reason you came out to see him. Seeing a park bench a ways off, you suggest that you sit down for a moment outside before heading back to the office. You start over to the bench, increasing your pace, and when you reach it, you stop and take a big breath. Looking around at the scenery, you change the subject, asking a direct question about his needs. You immediately sit down to listen.

What's Going On?    This simplistic scenario illustrates several steps in the process of pacing your customers. The first is to observe their pace by looking at mannerisms, breathing rate and intensity, and any other physical manifestations of mood—including loudness, speed and tone of voice, physical posture, and so on. Once you have identified a few of these mannerisms, you match them. Matching means gradually emulating your customers by matching your breath rate to theirs, matching their body language and voice tones, and so on. This must be done gradually and subtly; someone who realizes what you're doing will think you're parodying them and you'll blow it. Once you've matched them, you can gradually change the pace of each mannerism, and they will follow you. In essence you'll sync up, and then you can lead them into a receptive, communicative state.

In the example, you let the customer set the pace by heading outside. You probably peeled off your own jacket when he did and emulated his breezy, casual air as he told his assistant he'd be outside for a while. He continued to set the pace outside as you watched and learned his pattern of breaks, full breaths, and subject changes. Once you noticed the pattern, you matched it—then generated the next step yourself, heading to the bench, repeating the pattern, and going further into the subject.

To learn to pace you can practice anywhere with anyone. Pick one noticeable mannerism and match it, being careful not to exaggerate your attempts. Breathing is a good pacing tool to start with. Watch someone breathe and gradually match your breath to his or hers. Once you're matched, try gradually increasing or decreasing your rate to see if he or she follows. This also works well for voice tone and loudness. Your mother probably used expert pacing techniques to tone you down when you were loud and rowdy as a child. Even the expression "tone you down" implies pacing. If you were yelling, she'd yell, matching your volume and then bringing hers down, quieting you in the process and getting your attention.

Is pacing manipulative? It could be if you use it to make people do things they don't want to. A great deal of charisma—good and bad—comes from an individual's ability (usually unconscious) to pace the moods of others. Very charismatic leaders use this ability on a large scale to manipulate public opinion. In the case of Hitler, it was disastrous for the world; with his nemesis Churchill, it motivated an entire country to resist. Both used pacing to set the tone of their time.

As a salesperson, your use of tools like pacing has one goal: To increase rapport with customers and to help you understand their needs so you can fulfill them.

You might pace someone into a choice they don't want, but it will catch up to you in the long run.

Pacing in Groups     How do you pace a group during a sales meeting with more than one person? You cannot match several people at once with differing sets of signals. Fortunately you rarely need to try—most groups have already matched and paced themselves to one individual, usually the decision maker. As we've already seen, you are always selling to the one person who can make the choice, spend the money, and authorize the go-ahead. Your goal in a group presentation is always to find that person and present to him or her. The same goes for pacing. Find the leader's pace, match it, and you'll be in sync with the group.

## Representational Systems

Besides pacing and matching signals, another powerful technique for establishing rapport is to make sure you are communicating in the same language as your customer. In this case I'm not speaking of verbal languages based on geographic or ethnic roots; I'm speaking of the primary language we use to represent the world on a subconscious level. These languages are primarily visual (sight), auditory (sound), and kinesthetic (physical feeling and sensation). Each is a representational system, and most of us favor one over another.

Visual     Primarily visual thinkers, the majority at around 50 percent of the population, see mental images when they communicate and learn. You can identify them by listening and watching as they communicate. They will use visual metaphors such as "the big picture," "I see what you mean," "I can't picture it," "fill in the blanks" and other language full of visually descriptive words. They are sensitive to color, brightness, and appearance, so it is much easier to establish rapport with them if you match their visual system and use these kinds of image-oriented metaphors. Visually stimulating information displays work well as do graphs and charts rather than text.

AUDITORY Auditory representational system people are sound oriented. When you talk about the big bang theory, they don't make a picture of an exploding universe in their heads, they hear it. About 25 percent of the population, these auditory thinkers use language in a very different way from that of a visually oriented person. They vary their tone and pace, they use auditory metaphors such as "I like the sound of that" or "I hear you loud and clear," and they respond to auditory stimuli like exciting sound tracks, sonically varied presentations, or soothing background music. You can often pace them verbally by matching their tone and then varying it. They may respond better to text they can read and hear in their head than to graphs or images.

KINESTHETIC Kinesthetically oriented people are sensitive to touch, texture, heat and cold, vibrations, and other tactile input. They will touch and handle your product to the extent that even the heft and feel of a typed proposal may sway them. They speak in touchy-feely language that emphasizes physical response. "Give me a hands-on demonstration," "Let's hammer something out," "Keep in touch," or "Let's run over that one again until it's going smoothly." Obviously an emphasis on tactile, hands-on, try-it-and-see presentations is the best approach with these people.

MIXING REPRESENTATIONAL SYSTEMS   None of us is exclusively rooted in one system (with the possible exception of some autistic or developmentally disabled individuals). We all see, hear, and feel. We also use two other systems to a lesser degree, both of which can be very powerful. These are smell and taste. Smell in particular is a powerful trigger of memory and experience. If you sell products or services that touch these senses, like food or flowers, make sure you use these attributes to win over your customers.

The fact that we use all these systems means that your presentations and indeed every step of the sales process should contain descriptions and language in all three primary systems. As you meet and qualify, look for verbal and nonverbal cues that tell you how the people you're working with represent the world internally. Then use that knowledge to make your presentation in their language.

The effective use of representational systems is a powerful tool that is only beginning to be explored as a teaching and communications aid. As a sales tool, it is a great way to build rapport and avoid communications breakdowns. Often miscommunications occur because a very visual communicator is trying to use images to convey a concept to a very kinesthetic thinker. The result is similar to trying to sell in a foreign country through an interpreter: What you want to convey and what gets through may be very different things.

## Anchors

Anchors are a way of using the knowledge you've learned from pacing, matching, and understanding the representational system of your customer. An anchor is a cue that you place at a certain point. Perhaps you're making a strong point at a meeting—you've reached a critical part of your presentation and want to make sure that your audience will remember it. You'd also like to tap into that very focused attention later on. It is time to place an anchor. If your primary customer is visual, you may dramatically bring out a slide that is an intense color like red, a color not used previously in the presentation. The sudden appearance of an intense red image becomes associated in customers' minds with the information they are processing at that moment. Later, when you need their attention on that level again, what do you do? You call up your anchor by bringing out another powerful red image.

In the same situation with an auditory audience, you might clap your hands loudly or drop your voice to a whisper, silencing the room and focusing attention on the matter at hand. The next time you call up that anchor by clapping or whispering, you'll evoke the same response.

Kinesthetic anchors may be a pat on the shoulder or a sudden change of physical environment like going outside for a walk, as in the example at the beginning of the chapter. If you succeeded in making that sale, you might find that getting your client outdoors again in the future will predispose him to another sale.

■ ■ ■

These tools are basic to all human communications, which means that you can learn by observing others and trying them out in a variety of situations. Any place you can unobtrusively observe and listen will help you start to recognize the signals that can tell you more about how someone thinks and processes information.

There are inevitably questions about the propriety of using these hidden or subconscious tools to achieve your own ends. My experience is that when you achieve rapport with people it is an empathic event; you feel and experience their view of the world. This is an expansive learning experience that brings you closer to others. Instead of being a manipulative out-sider, you enter into their world and become more able to offer them valuable resources and solutions.

# CHAPTER 25

# IMPROVING
# YOUR PRODUCT

If you've been practicing any of the skills and techniques in *Sales for the Self-Employed* out in the real world, you may be discovering that your products or services are not perfect. In fact, if you have managed to see them from your customers' point of view, you may have discovered substantial flaws or weaknesses—or even unexpected areas of strength. A feature that you had little interest in may be getting more attention than you expected. Another may not get any response or may require some fine-tuning to fit the needs of your customers.

Another result of getting out and selling is often the discovery of new products. You learn of a need that you can fulfill, a classic formula for business success.

Ideally, these new products are extensions or specialized versions of what you already do or sell, meaning you can make additional sales to proven customers.

The widespread and instant availability of inform ation means that the entire concept of a *product* is changing. Once you picked a product of the shelf and made use of it as it was. Now products are often customized to each customer's specific needs, either by the customer, the seller, or a third party. Digital versions of information products like software, books, training systems, music, video, and film can all be manipulated in ways that were inaccessible to most of us a few years ago. As a writer of books, I deliver a completed product that is printed and sold as is. In a few years, my readers may subscribe to my knowledge on a particular subject and download or access only those parts relevant to their needs. They may buy a custom laser-printed book or simply use their own digital viewer.

The important point and inherent change involved for self-employed people is a major one. Our very small businesses have been dependent on the resources of others to distribute our message, our skills, and our products. This is changing in ways that may mean that you can compete with or even beat much larger companies at their own game. Concepts like the creation of virtual businesses that exist only in a digital conferencing environment and can be put together only for one job or customer are becoming normal in some fields.

This disengagement from traditional continuing and growing enterprises is difficult for the typical employee-type worker to cope with. However, for a self-employed person, it is often the norm. As a result, many of us are in a much better position for the future than our corporate counterparts. We may not have the paychecks, but we do have the flexibility, a key asset today.

The ability to sell yourself is essential to survival in rapidly changing situations. In fact, your ability to sell and the ability to customize your product are two huge advantages in today's information-driven economy. Average salary workers seldom sell anything—and when they do, they have little training or experience to fall back on. You, on the other hand, are out there every day selling as a matter of survival.

## CUSTOMIZING YOUR PRODUCTS

Most of us offer products that fit our set of skills and experiences. We offer a service or product based on what we know and then seek a target market for those products, as described in Chapter 3. When you're starting out and have little customer contact and input, this approach may be a necessary one. However, after you've tested the waters and begun to interact regularly with your customers, this can and should change. Selling is in part an information-gathering process. Once you've acquired enough information, you use it to make the sale.

Using information only to consummate one sale is a poor use of your time. Taking that information and using it to improve or enhance the overall salability of your products is a much more effective strategy. For instance, if you are selling kitchen cabinets and your customers tell you over and over again that they are having problems scheduling the construction of their new kitchen, you may have identified a new product area. Perhaps you should consider offering a consulting service to help them find and schedule workers and purchases. Or if you don't want to get into that end of the business, consider adding a report or planner for kitchen construction as an added freebie with a cabinet purchase. An incentive like this may be the benefit that gets you the job over another bidder.

Product enhancement should be a never-ending process. Mature products may actually be on their last legs. By continually improving and upgrading, you open up new business—and you can sell the upgraded product to existing customers. Many software companies have generated very successful repeat business doing just that. Consider these options for enhancing your current products and services:

■ *Improved packaging.* This means everything from a nicer bag in a store to a new truck sign for a landscaper or contractor. It may mean going to recyclable materials or packaging that offers more protection or easier access.

■ *Improved support services.* Consider offering a contractual follow-up and customer service option when you sell a service or complex product. This may involve selling a few hours of your time monthly on a retainer basis or having you come in for a regular evaluation every six months. In my consulting business, I usually include several hours of consulting time when I sell a marketing or business plan. Customers can bring me in any time within the next year for any questions or upgrades they want. The time limit is necessary to increase the value of the service. I also remind customers about the time if they haven't used it. This is good service and serves to put me back in touch with past clients.

■ *Related supplies or refills.* If your business or product uses inventory that gets used up over time like fertilizer, paper, paint, and so on, consider offering these related products for sale along with your landscaping, printing, or painting business. Buy wholesale and mark the products up. The advantages to the buyers are one-stop shopping and your inside knowledge of what is best for their needs.

■ *Other people's services.* Do the projects you work on involve other self-employed people? If so, you can handle the customer relations for them and mark up their services. For example, when someone hires a graphic design firm to create a brochure, chances are that as part of the package the design firm will subcontract parts of the project to a writer, a photographer, an output service, and a printer. These suppliers give the design firm a price break because they didn't need to spend time and money to get the job. The design firm charges for its time coordinating things and marks up the other services. The customer gets a coordinated project and saves a lot of time trying to deal with many unfamiliar aspects of the project.

■ *Long-term commitment.* Cash flow is a big problem with many self-employed businesses because we tend to go from having a lot of work all at once to having nothing to do but hunt. You can even out this cyclical business flow by getting retainers from regular customers. You offer a package rate for a bundle of hours or a service each month in exchange for a regular contractual arrangement. Florists may agree to supply a restaurant with flowers twice a week for a monthly fee. While they make less money on the flowers, they have a regular and predictable flow of cash to pay bills during slow periods.

■ *Future versions of your product.* Chances are pretty good that you will not be in the same business five years from now. Your interests will change, the market will change, and the products you offer and compete with will change. You should stay abreast of new developments in your business area and watch for new trends and breakthroughs in technology or processes that you can be the first to offer your customers. As an expert, you will not have the steep learning curve necessary to develop skills with new products. However, you must stay up to speed with new technology to keep this edge. This can put you in the enviable position of being on the spot with the right knowledge and skills when a new development becomes the product everyone wants but few people offer. There is always a brief period in these situations when it is a seller's market—meaning opportunities for greater profits and more interesting work.

## DEVELOPING NEW PRODUCTS

It is common for self-employed people to fear new products or to stubbornly stick with what has always worked for them. The problem with sticking to the good old ways of doing things is that they are only the "good old ways" for your older customers and they only remain the "good old ways" until something better comes along. I have clear memories of my art director friends shying away from the desktop publishing revolution in the eighties. The common refrain was that it would never work as well as actually pasting up ads and graphics on a board. Those who eventually jumped on the computer revolution thrived; those who didn't found themselves replaced by young designers who started on computers and had no such prejudices about new technology.

Planning to enter a new product area is also a way to breathe new life into a stale business. Often, after the initial thrill of self-employment wears off, we are more prosperous but less challenged by our work. Taking the plunge into a new product, skill, or service is not like starting over. The essential skills you've developed—including sales—remain with you. In fact, you'll get up and running much faster because you won't make all the same mistakes again. While it is common to think that you're too old or established to make big changes, the reality is that you are far better equipped with experience to do so. You just have to develop a little of the blind faith that a newbie gets by on and supplement it with your experience.

Developing new or additional products is an evolutionary process rather than a creation process. We seldom stop what we're doing and build a new life out of whole cloth. Even if you completely change horses, your riding skills cannot be taken away and they will affect your new venture. To start a product development process, look at what you do now and how you can leverage those skills into new, more interesting and profitable products. Consider these options:

■ *Spin-offs.* Branching out into related products or services is an excellent way to leverage your sales efforts from the past by offering new but related products to your current customers. One recent example is the trend to put water purification systems in homes. My plumber has added the sales and installation of these systems to his business. When someone calls him in for a repair, he is in a perfect position to sell these related products.

■ *Information packages.* You can publish your own expert information to sell to interest groups, associations, and potential customers that you cannot sell to personally. Today this instant publishing may mean laser-printed reports, e-mail newsletters, audio or videotapes, and other products easily duplicated in short runs. The information must be of high value and timeliness in order to command a high enough price to justify the marketing cost. Generally reports or training services should sell for at least $100 to be profitable. The actual cost of manufacture is negligible; it is the marketing required that drives the price up. The nice thing about these types of products is that you only do the work once and then sell it over and over again.

Be creative when seeking a market. I have a friend who writes a real estate newsletter. He doesn't sell it to individuals; he sells it to brokers who customize it for their market. He gets a high price and only has to market it to an easily targeted group of prospects.

■ *Training.* You're an expert in a number of things—starting and running a business, setting goals, doing various expert things (your business), and so on. You can train others to do these things through seminars, classes, the Internet, and other media. Often this will lead to sales as potential customers attend these events to check you out rather than to do it themselves.

Seminar selling is a potent tool for finding highly qualified customers. Financial planners use it all the time by offering seminars on retirement planning, mutual funds, and other topics. They offer valuable information and then do a sales presentation at the end after establishing their creditability. Almost any business can offer an introductory seminar to sell products and prospect for customers.

■ *Inventions.* You are in an ideal place to invent new products within your specialty. After all, you work with the same tools and problems every day and know them intimately. If you identify a way to save time, money, or stress, invent a solution and sell it to others in your business. You don't have to be a rocket scientist—most inventions are simple, and most inventors were simply seeking a more efficient way to do things. If you think you've got a good idea, sketch it out and go to a patent attorney for an opinion before you spend money. Don't worry about confidentiality; any reputable patent attorney is a safe person to share an idea with. Stay away from companies catering to inventors, though—they are notorious for being expensive scams.

■ ■ ■

The best product improvements you can make are those suggested by your customers. When someone suggests an improvement or a new use for your skills, implement that suggestion and keep your sources informed as to your progress. They'll take a personal interest and help you as an informal partner. Your willingness to change and your open attitude to suggestions are also key aspects of making continued sales to all of your customers. Always offering new and enhanced products tells them that you're interested in constantly improving your business—and theirs.

# CHAPTER 26

# SALES
# TOOLS

In Chapter 3, we looked at various prospecting tools you can use to help you find motivated and qualified buyers for your products and services. There are also powerful tools available to help you improve your sales skills and profits. These sales tools are rapidly changing as the ways we communicate change. In this chapter, we take a look at a few essential tools for managing the sales part of your life as a self-employed person.

## TIME MANAGEMENT

Time management is such a common business buzzword these days that many of us tend to ignore it as a trendy subject for seminars and consultants. Yet time is our most valuable and limited resource. It is also the great equalizer—no one has more or less time available than you. As a sales tool, time management is valuable because it helps create urgency, it sets prices, and it keeps you in regular contact with your customers. The urgency is generated by scheduling and deadlines that serve as motivation to take action. The prices are based on the value of both your time and your customer's time. If you provide a product that saves time, allowing people to pursue more profitable things, you have a powerful argument for their purchase of that product. Setting up a regular schedule of customer contact keeps you on track with your selling and ensures that you don't forget important customers from your past.

The key to effective time management is habit. Actions become habits when you perform them regularly. Before you give yourself time management tasks like scheduling or To Do lists, you have to set aside time to make these actions habits. Time management studies show that, on average, you must perform an action daily for 21 days before it becomes habitual or automatic. Therefore the first time management task you should assign yourself is to agree to perform each action daily for at least a month before giving up on it.

The primary time management tool is the planner. This can be a printed calendar, a book of days, a computer program, or any other place dedicated to planning your use of time and readily accessible. My personal preference is a planner and calendar book that has a page dedicated to each day. Because it does not require power and is portable and instantly accessible, it works better than electronic or software versions for my needs. Whatever you use, the key to all planner use is regularity. Spend 10 to 15 minutes each morning with your planner, scheduling appointments, reviewing upcoming actions, or simply making notes about new projects, ideas, or recent insights.

This daily meeting with your planner is a chance to consider where your business is going and how it fits in with your personal life. It's an opportunity for reflection. The notes you take and reviews you do will make a big difference in how organized you are and appear to be to your customers. Take 15 minutes a day for a month and try it. You'll find it's habit forming.

## VOLUNTEER WORK

Volunteering your services is a powerful sales tool when you choose to work where you can make the most impact. Volunteering on projects where you can work alongside potential customers puts you in a work situation together and builds respect and rapport. Often I hear complaints about old boy networks and inside connections making it impossible to reach certain customers. These networks often depend on membership in community and business associations and participation in their activities and programs. All it takes to get inside is getting to know people on a level of mutual interest. Volunteering is a good way to reach those inaccessible insiders. The key is not just joining—you must participate, work alongside people, to become an insider yourself.

## PUBLIC SPEAKING

The alleged number one fear of most people—public speaking—is an invaluable skill for improving your ability to communicate. There is nothing like the intensity involved in telling a compelling story in public and moving people to action or sympathy. Public speaking forces you to organize your thoughts in an easily understood manner and helps you polish your delivery. The best way to learn is through membership in an organization like Toastmasters, which exists both to train speakers and to help its members make connections with other business and community-minded people. As scary as public speaking may seem, you can not only learn to do it—you may even get to like it. Once you're an accomplished speaker, you'll see your sales ability take a quantum leap. It is a very compressed form of skill building.

## CUSTOMER DATABASE

By now you probably know that I consider a computer an essential tool for any one-person business. Fortunately, you don't need the latest high-powered flavor of the week. Any machine built in the last five years will run 99 percent of the software you're likely to need, including customer database software. The advantages over rotary files and 3 × 5 cards are significant. Setting up a database is extremely easy—just get one of the many excellent programs available, and it will walk even the most computer illiterate person through the process. The important thing to remember about computers is that newer technology means more ease of use rather than more complexity. The best software is also the easiest to use.

A typical customer database program has a file for each customer containing any and all relevant information on that person. Besides putting in all the normal contact and background info, you can customize the files to show any kind of category you want—and then search by category. You can also add notes and insert reminders to yourself that tell you when it's time to make a call or send a note. The software also offers customized sales letters, label printing, and a host of other useful functions. Once you've entered your customers' names, it's simple to keep the file up to date.

The advantage to computer use is the power of knowledge about your business that it makes available. When the phone rings, you can quickly access everything you know about the customer and check progress on estimates, previous experience, invoices, and other data. It gives you the speed and flexibility of a much larger business with numerous employees without the cost or responsibility.

## EXERCISE AND NUTRITION

Yes, you read that right. How you look and feel has a direct effect on your ability to sell. A healthy lifestyle is obvious to your customers and gives you the clarity to pick up on the many messages involved in any sales situation. Excessive consumption of anything from fried foods to alcohol or drugs blunts your ability to focus and slows your response time. A few minutes spent exercising will give you more energy than ten cups of joe—and eating less and healthier food will make you stronger and happier . . . and more persuasive in every sales meeting.

## AN OPEN MIND

This one should be obvious—but a closed mind is probably the single most common problem for self-employed people trying to sell their work. We walk into a meeting with preconceptions about ourselves and the customer, preconceptions that limit our ability to perceive. My assumption that a potential customer is seeking a particular service from me may mean that I automatically launch into a presentation for that service. It is amazing how often our preconceptions are wrong. Right or wrong, they serve to limit our thinking. Try to leave your thoughts aside when entering a sales situation and expect the unexpected. You'll be more prepared to take advantage of it.

Open-mindedness can result in bigger and more profitable sales. Often customers may be testing the waters for a bigger project or purchase by getting together to discuss something more limited. If you limit your focus to the product they expressed an initial interest in, you may not hear the entire message they're sending. This has happened to many of the small business owners I work with. They go into a meeting with an assumption about what will happen, only to find that things are very different. Many times customers may need to divulge confidential needs or plans and want to be sure they can trust you before doing so.

## FAST RESPONSE

Fast response is a potent sales tool because so few of your competitors use it. Fast response simply means getting back to your customers on each and every request for information or assistance quickly. How quickly? Faster than they are used to. There is nothing more frustrating than to ask for a quote or bid and then not hear anything for days or even weeks. Your job as a businessperson is to be able to assemble your resources quickly and respond professionally. A fast response may not only get you the sale, it can eliminate some price challenges from your slower competition—you may get the job before they get the bid out, or you may get it in the face of a cheaper bid because your demonstrated speed is valuable to your customer.

## SHOP TALK

Shop talk is conversation with other business owners about running a business. It is also a meeting ground for communications with your competition. The reality about small business competition is that every business has different strengths and expertise. Your competition may not really be after the same things you are, and even if they are, the world is a very big place with plenty of customers to go around. If that is not the case in your business, then you should look at your business carefully and evaluate its necessity. In the meantime, get out and talk to others to learn, pick up information, and make contacts. A lot of referrals will come from fellow business owners who not only understand their value but hope for the return of the favor.

## SALES TOOLS FOR TOMORROW

With technology changing our work world at an extremely rapid pace, will your sales skills become outdated the way those of the archetypical crooked used car vendor have? The primary change coming into the next century involves communications. The world becomes a smaller place with each breakthrough. Things that seemed far-fetched in our youth are commonplace—cell phones, e-mail, the Web with all the access to information it offers. New technology is making videoconferencing available to even the smallest business, enabling you to carry your selling ability to any customer anywhere, instantly.

The ramifications of this are startling, especially for the small business owner. To put it simply, we stand at the edge of the greatest sales opportunity in history, one that seems designed for the self-employed. Instead of looking for prospects in a universe limited by our access and physical ability to interact with our customers, we can reach out to virtually anyone. This means that you can be very specific in your market and your product selection and still have hundreds, thousands, or millions of qualified prospects.

One early indicator of this was the explosion in newsletter publishing during the seventies and early eighties. These newsletters often targeted extremely narrow interest groups, charging very high annual subscription rates for current, inside, and highly valued information. They were made possible by the advent of database marketing, which made it possible to sift through lists of prospects to create a customer list of people who shared a unique set of interests and needs. In some cases, the publisher of a newsletter could have positive response rates for subscription offers of up to 90 percent, a return unheard of previously.

Now these newsletters are obsolete—they're being replaced by Internet sites that make the same specialized information instantly accessible to anyone and make it possible to get current news every minute. The Internet has also lifted database marketing to a new level of simplicity, making it possible to tap into thousands of interest groups through the search engines built into the system. One person tapping into the Internet with a personal computer suddenly has access to resources that until recently cost thousands of dollars and took complex skills and much time to acquire. And these resources have another very interesting aspect: They are completely democratic in a way that transcends education, culture, economic status, geographic location, and every other traditional definition of social power. Anyone can get there with readily accessible tools.

The interesting thing about this change is that simply putting up a Web site or searching the Net for interest groups is not enough in itself to ensure business success. You still have to market to tell people about your solutions and then sell them just as you would in a face-to-face medium. And that means going through each step of the process, whether you do it with an interactive e-mail questionnaire attached to a Web site, in a chat room, or via correspondence. You still meet, qualify, present, and close.

■ ■ ■

These tools are only a few of the many tools available to improve your sales skills. The interesting thing about selling is that you can practice anywhere with anyone because selling is one-on-one communications with a fellow human. Listening and problem-solving skills are a part of everyday life, and simply becoming conscious of them and practicing will make a big improvement in your sales and your life.

# RESOURCES

## BOOKS

### General Business

Hawken, Paul. *Growing a Business.* New York: Simon & Schuster, 1987. One of the best books out there for anyone starting a business. Entertaining and realistic. Highly recommended.

Bermont, Hubert. *How to Become a Successful Consultant in Your Own Field.* Rocklin, California: Prima, 1995. One of the best books on being self-employed I've come across. Bermont believes (and backs it up) that seminars are the way to sell expert services.

## General Marketing

Levinson, Jay Conrad. *Guerrilla Marketing.* Boston: Houghton Mifflin, 1984.

———, *Guerrilla Marketing Attack.* Boston: Houghton Mifflin, 1989.

The Guerrilla series includes a number of excellent general small business marketing books. They are based on the premise that a creative small business marketer can beat out competition big and small by being innovative. Levinson gives many specific examples of tactics and strategy.

## Direct Response and Direct Mail

Bustiner, Irving. *Mail Order Selling: How to Market Almost Anything by Mail* (3rd ed.). New York: Wiley, 1995. A classic on using mail order that has many techniques you'll find useful even if you're not a mail order business, particularly on the use of classified advertising.

Geller, Lois K. *Response!: The Complete Guide to Profitable Direct Marketing.* New York: Free Press, 1996. A guide to small business direct marketing that covers everything from copy techniques to online sales.

## Sales

Gallagher, Bill, Orvel Ray Wilson, and Jay Conrad Levinson, *Guerrilla Selling.* Boston, Houghton Mifflin, 1992. Another Guerrilla book with a good—though often idealized—approach to sales.

Girard, Joe, with Robert L. Shook. *How to Close Every Sale.* New York: Warner Books, 1989. Joe is a legendary car salesman who sold over 13,000 cars in ten years, an amazing feat. His techniques are valuable for their emphasis on developing customer relationships that lead to repeat sales.

Schiffman, Stephan. *Cold Call Selling Techniques (That Really Work)* (3rd ed.). Adams, 1990. Picking up the phone is the number one way to build your business. This short book takes the mystery and much of the fear out of the process.

Boyan, Lee. *Successful Cold Call Selling* (2nd ed.). New York: AMACOM, 1989. One hundred ideas, scripts, and examples of how others use the phone as a sales tool.

Gilleland, Karen. *450 Best Sales Letters For Every Selling Situation.* Englewood Cliffs, N.J.: Prentice Hall, 1991. Sales letters can get things started, resolve problems, and bring old customers back. Use these as templates for your own.

## *Advertising*

Bruneau, Edmund A. *Rx (Prescription) for Advertising.* Boston: Boston Books, 1986. The book for the business owner considering the use of advertising to promote business. How to deal with writers, artists, agencies, media, and so on—written in a down-to-earth, expert voice.

## Invisible Selling

Bandler, Richard, and John Grinder. *Frogs into Princes: Neuro-Linguistic Programming*. Moab, Utah: Real People Press, 1979. NLP is a new way of looking at the entire process of communicating including pacing, anchoring, representational systems, and other breakthrough models for learning about human interaction. This is one of the titles that started it off, a transcript of a very entertaining and enlightening seminar by two giants in the field.

## Developing New Products

Tripp, Alan R. *Millions from the Mind*. New York: AMACOM, 1992. In spite of the silly title, this is the best book I've found on developing, protecting, and marketing your ideas and inventions. If you're afraid someone will steal your great idea, read this book.

## MAGAZINES AND PERIODICALS

*Inc. Magazine*. A source of useful tips and advice from your peers. As with any of these resources, even one small but profitable idea easily justifies the price of a subscription or book.

*In Business*, J. G. Press, Emmaus, Pennsylvania. Oriented to companies with under 25 employees, including many one-person businesses.

## Miscellaneous

*The Small Business Administration.* Check your phone book under Federal Government to find the nearest office. They have many useful, free publications, can offer excellent help with planning and financing, and may hook you up with a Service Corps Of Retired Executives (SCORE) mentor who can help you find your way through the ins and outs of business management.

# INDEX

**A**

Ability to pay, 155–156
Action-oriented words in business
  description, 34
Advertising, 40–41
  frequency of, 41
Age of customers, 17
AIDA formula, 145–146
Alcohol use, 294
Appointments, 32–33, 57–65
  confirmation of, 60
  ending the appointment, 63
  first contact, arranging at, 51–52
  follow-up to, 63–64
  interruptions to, 58–59
  negative reaction to, 64
  preparation for, 59–61
  rehearsal of, 60
  review of, 63–64

stage fright, 60–61
time slots designated for,
  58–59
undivided attention during, 59
Archimedes, 88
Attention
  qualifying customers and,
    169–170
  in trial close, 189
Auctions, 167, 263
Auditory impressions, 72
  anchors in, 275–276
  in meet and greet, 148–150
  as representational system, 273

**B**

Bandler, Richard, 268
Beginning-to-end responsibility, 234

Benefits-oriented work in business
    description, 34
Bermont, Hubert, 85
Bird-dog programs, 248, 254–255
  ground rules for, 255
  key to, 255
Bottom line in negotiations, 262–263
Brochures, 37
  capability brochures, 137–138
  direct mail of, 38
  in requests for proposals
    (RFPs), 224
Budgets
  for portfolios, 136
  sales plan including, 95–96
Business cards, 35–37
Business name, 34–35
Buyers, qualified, 154–159

## C

Calendars, 290–291
Canned spiels, 182
Capability brochures, 137–138
Capitalism, 261
Case study presentations, 130–132
CD-ROM, mailing lists on, 29
Cellular phones, 297
Change-of-life proposals, 231–232
Churchill, Winston, 271
Classified ads, 41
Closing, 9, 11, 191–198
  buy, agreement to, 192–193
  defined, 192
  delivery of goods, 196
  good closers, 197–198
  good-faith deposit, 195
  price, agreement on, 194
  time frame, agreement on, 196

  value, agreement on, 193–194
  in writing, 195–196
Cold calls, 31–33
  examples of, 48–50
  press kit in, 40
Commission pay structure, 9
Commitment to sales, 47
Communications, 99–105
  closing and, 197–198
  failure to communicate, 102–103
  focusing on, 170
  listening and, 104–105
  meet and greet via, 143
Competition, persistence and, 77–78
Compromise in negotiation, 262
Computer database of customers,
  292–294
Conferences, 42
Confirmation of appointments, 60
Conscious selling, 69–71
Consistent message in presentation,
  180–181
Consultants, problem-solving by, 108
Contacts. *See also* First contact
  maintaining contact with
    customers, 220
  sales plan, list of contacts in, 91–92, 94
Content, defined, 101
Contracts
  on closing, 195–196
  proposals as, 227
Copywriters for portfolios, 135
Core problems
  in qualifying customers, 159–160
  in trial close, 187–188
Creative listening, 54–55
Customers. *See also* First contact;
    Qualifying customers
  attributes of, 17
  convincing people to buy, 110–111

database of, 292–294
forever, 211–212
mannerisms of, 270–271
passions of, 126
past customers, contact of, 219–220
personal investment by, 47–52
presentation research and, 125–128
profiling customers, 16–17
ten prospects for success, 18–19
Customizing
portfolios, 134–136
products, 279–283

## D

Database of customers, 292–294
Daydreams, 120
Deadlines, 290
Decision makers, 155
self-esteem and, 167–168
Delivery, 199–207
attitude and, 199–200
closing and, 196
completed work, 206
small town environment and,
201–202
Demographic mailing lists, 29
Demonstrations of product, 139,
206–207
Deposits, good-faith, 195
Desires, 115–121
customizing presentation to, 129
needs and, 116–119
Direct mail, 38–39
Direct-response marketing, 38
Disassociation techniques, 73–75
Display ads, 41
"Don't take it personally," 85–86
Drug use, 294

## E

Eastman Kodak, 181
Education of customers, 17
800 telephone numbers
direct mail including, 39
E-mail, 297
direct mail including address, 39
information packages on, 285
meet and greet via, 143
sales over, 62
Estimates
appointments, use at, 62
at presentations, 179–180
Ethnic background of customers, 17
Exercise
and motivation, 239–241
as sales tool, 294
Eye contact, 147

## F

Faking rapport, 266
Fast response, 295–296
Favors as incentives, 249–250
Fear, 79–86
communication and, 100
"Don't take it personally," 85–86
first contact and, 45
goals dissipating, 84
motivation and, 79–80
negative motivation, 81–83
presentation, fear and, 82
prospecting and, 27–28
rejection, fear of, 84–86
trial close and, 185–186
Features-benefits comparison, 21–24
hanging features without
benefits, 24

First contact, 45–56. *See also* Meet
   and greet
   bonds, establishing, 52–53
   creative listening and, 54–55
   example of, 48–50
   networking and, 53–54
   objective of, 51
   sales plan planning for, 95
First impressions, 144–145
Five-step sales process, 7–12
Follow-ups, 211–220. *See also*
   Referrals
   to appointments, 63–64
   future sales and, 213–216
   planning for, 212–213
   on proposals, 226–227
   support services as, 281
   thank yous, 218–219
Freebies, 183–184
   as incentives, 252–254
   negotiation in, 258
Full-sensory approach to
   presentation, 72
Future sales, 213–216


**G**

Gift certificates, 248
Gifts as thank yous, 218–219
Goals
   fear, dissipation of, 84
   of first contact, 51
   in meet and greet situation,
      142, 149
   positive goals, 83
Good-faith deposit, 195
Graphic designers
   business cards, design for, 36
   for portfolios, 135

Greeting cards, 38
Grinder, John, 268
Group presentations, 138
   pacing in, 272


**H**

Habits, 290
Handshakes, 147–148
Hanging features without benefits, 24
Hidden agenda, 113–114
Hitler, Adolf, 271
Hobbies and motivation, 242–243
Home shopping channel product
   demonstrations, 139
*How to Succeed as a Consultant in Your
   Own Field* (Bermont), 85


**I**

Ideas
   questions related to, 164–166
   in spec proposals, 230
Identifying best customers, 28–29
Improving products, 277–287
Impulse purchases, 119
Incentives, 245–256
   to buy, 252–254
   enticement of, 246–247
   favors as, 249–250
   "free" as, 252–253
   indulgences as, 247–248
   money as, 248–249, 251–252
   motivation and, 244
   self-motivation and, 250–251
   time incentives, 251–252
   for yourself, 250–252
Income range of customers, 17

Indulgences as incentives, 247–248
Infomercials, 139
Information-gathering stage, 70
Information packages, 285
Informed beginners, 124–125
Initial contact. *See* First contact
Integration of selling, 67–68
Interest group membership
    of customers, 17
Internal dialogue, 169–170
    settling down, 236
Internal quiet, 241–242
Internet, 297–298
    features-benefits comparison
        and, 24
    portfolio, Web site in, 133
    training others on, 285
Inventions, 286
Inventorying sales abilities, 113
Invisible selling, 265–276
Invitations, 38

**J**

Japan, National Treasure status
    in, 238
Job description of customers, 17

**K**

Key people, referrals from, 217–218
Kickbacks, 254
Kinetic impressions, 72
    anchors in, 287
    in meet and greet, 147–148
    portfolios and, 133
    as representational system,
        273–274

Kirby vacuum cleaner
    demonstrations, 139
Knowledge and motivation, 237–239

**L**

Learning to sell, 69–70
Leverage
    product leverage, 214–215
    sales plan and, 88–89
Lifestyle of customers, 20
List brokers, 29
Listening
    closing and, 197–198
    communication and, 104–105
    creative listening, 54–55
    internal dialogue and, 169–170
    qualifying customers and, 169
Lists of customers, 29
Logos, 35
Long-distance selling, 60–61
Long-term commitment and
        products, 282
Looky-lous, 156–158
Luxuries as incentives, 247–248

**M**

Mailing lists, 29
    contracts with members of, 29
Mannerisms of customer, 270–271
Materials for presentations, 128–139
Material worth, 166–167
Meditation and motivation,
        241–242
Meet and greet, 9, 10, 141–151
    AIDA formula, 145–146
    first impressions, 144–145

Meet and greet *continued*
  goals of, 142
  visual impressions in, 146–147
Monday morning sales
    meeting, 9
Money. *See also* Budgets; Prices
  as incentive, 248–249, 251–252
  in negotiations, 263–264
  qualifying customers and,
    162–164
  questions about, 157
  trial close and, 185
Motivation, 233–244
  adversity and, 102
  for cold calls, 33
  developing motivational process,
    235–244
  fear and, 79–80
  incentives and, 244
  knowledge and, 237–239
  meditation and, 241–242
  mental component to, 240–241
  negative motivation, 81–83
  outside interests and, 242–243
  perspective, loss of, 242
  physical well-being and, 239–241

**N**

Name of business, 34–35
Natural sales talent, 5–6
Needs, 115–121
  customizing presentation to, 129
  desires and, 116–119
  discovery of, 119–120
Negotiation, 257–264
  decision for, 258–259
  everything is negotiable, 261–262
  information and, 259–260

offer in, 260–261
  risk management in, 262–264
  time and, 259–260
Networking, 42
  first contact and, 53–54
New products, 277–287
Newsletters, 285, 297–298
News media
  communication and, 100
  press releases, 39–41
Niche markets, 90–91, 94
Nonverbal cues, 274
Nutrition, 294

**O**

Objections of in presentation, dealing
    with, 182–184
Objectives. *See* Goals
Offer in negotiation, 260–261
Office, features-benefits comparison
    and, 23
One-sentence business description,
    33–34
  in first contact, 51
Open-mindedness, 294–295
Oral contracts on closing,
    195–196
Order takers, 15–16
Outline of sales plan, 93–96

**P**

Pacing of sales, 269–272
  in groups, 272
Packaging improvements, 280
Patent attorneys, 286
Perfect world questions, 166

Persistence
  as number one requirement, 233
  qualifying customers and, 169
  as sales skill, 77–78
Personal appearance, 146–147
Personal contacts, 30
Personal investment
  by business owner, 47
  by customers, 47–52
Photography for portfolios, 135
Physical well-being and motivation, 239–241
Pitch. *See* Presentations
Planners, 290–291
Portfolios, 37–38, 112, 132–138
  appointments, use at, 60
  budgets for, 136
  capability brochures in, 137–138
  customized portfolios, 134–136
  definition of, 133
  product demonstrations, 139
  relevance of, 133
  résumés for, 136–137
Positive motivation, 81–83
Positive thinking, 83
Postcards, 38
Potential market, 13–14
Preparation for appointments, 59–61
Prequalifying prospects, 33
Presentations, 9, 10–11, 123–140,
    173–184. *See also* Group presen-
    tations; Portfolios
  appointments, use at, 60
  assembling materials for, 129–130
  capabilities, overview of, 176–177
  case study presentations, 130–132
  estimates at, 179–180
  full-sensory approach to, 72
  materials for, 128–139
  needs and, 118

  objections, dealing with, 182–184
  pattern model for, 174
  personal background, overview of,
    174–176
  price, discussion of, 177–178
  quotes at, 179–180
  rehearsal of, 75–77, 93, 95
  research for, 124–128
  sales plan including, 92, 95
  shutting up after, 178–179
  solutions, overview of, 177–178
  store and retail presentations, 180
  style of, 180–182
  tailoring product presentation, 21
  writing, deals in, 179
Press kits, 40
Press releases, 39–40
  angle in, 40
Prices
  closing, agreement on
    price and, 194
  negotiation in, 258
  objections to, 183
  presentation, discussion of, 177–178
  in project proposal, 225
  proposal pricing, 222
  value, agreement on, 193–194
Problems and solutions, 6–7, 107–114.
    *See also* Core problems
  in case study presentation, 13
  challenges, problems as, 108–109
  convincing people to buy, 110–111
  identifying solutions, 111–113
  presentation, solutions at, 177–178
  products as solutions, 20–24,
    113–114
  sizzle and the steak, 109–110
Process
  defined, 101
  of selling, 7–12

Product demonstrations, 139
Products. *See also* Delivery
  considerations for delivery of, 203–204
  customizing products, 279–283
  demonstration of, 206–207
  demonstrations, 139
  developing new products, 283–286
  follow-up products, 214–215
  future versions of, 282–283
  ideas and, 164–165
  improving products, 277–287
  information packages, 285
  inventing new products, 286
  leverage, 214–215
  long-term commitment and, 282
  packaging improvements, 280
  as solutions, 20–24, 113–114
  spec product proposals, 229–230
  spin-offs of, 284–285
  time problems and, 161–162
Professional communicators, 55–56
Profiling customers, 16–17
Projects
  completed work, 205–206
  proposals for, 225–226
  spec project proposals, 215–216, 228–231
  time and sale of, 160–161
Promises in presentation, 181
Proposals, 221–232. *See also* Requests
    for proposals (RFPs)
  appointments, use at, 62
  change-of-life proposals, 231–232
  follow-up on, 226–227
  formats for, 225
  pricing in, 222
  project proposals, 225–226
  promises in, 227–228

  spec project proposals, 215–216, 228–231
  timing of, 226
Prospecting, 14–15
  one-sentence business description, 33–34
  process, 28–30
  relationship selling and, 19–20
  tool kit for, 30–43
  tools for, 27–43
Publicity, 39–40
  press releases, 39–40
Public speaking, 99–100
  as sales tool, 292

# Q

Qualifying customers, 9, 10, 153–171
  ability to pay, 155–156
  buyers, qualified, 154–159
  continuing with uncomfortable situation, 158–159
  core problems, identification of, 159–160
  idea-related questions, 164–166
  listening and, 169
  looky-lous, 156–158
  money and, 162–164
  objects in presentation and, 183
  perfect world questions, 166
  pricing differences and, 194
  problem-solving and, 207–208
  for product sales, 161–162
  for project sales, 160–161
  self-esteem issue, 166–168
  time problems, 160–162
Questions in presentation, dealing with, 182–184

Quotes
appointments, use at, 62
at presentations, 179–180

# R

Rapport, 266–276
anchors and, 275–276
pacing and, 269–272
representational systems and, 272–275
science of developing, 268
Rarity and value, 102
Rate structures, 181
Reactions to selling situation, 120
Recognition as incentive, 247–248
Referrals, 216–218. *See also* Bird-dog programs
by customers, 19
favors, referrals as, 249
psychology of, 217
to qualified buyers, 155
shop talk and, 296
Refills of products, 281
Rehearsal
of appointment, 60
of meet and greet, 148–149
of presentation, 75–77, 93, 95
Rejection, fear of, 84–86
Relationship selling, 19–20
Religious background of customers, 17
Representational systems, 272–275
mixing of, 274–275
Requests for proposals (RFPs), 137, 221, 222–225
brochures in, 224
governments using, 223

Research
appointments, customer research for, 59–60
motivation and, 235
for presentation, 124–128
Résumés, 112
in portfolios, 136–137
Retail presentations, 138–139
RFPs. *See* Requests for proposals (RFPs)
Risk management in negotiation, 262–264
Role-playing training, 76–77

# S

Sales letters, 38
with project proposal, 225–226
Sales plan
budgets in, 95–96
first contact, planning the, 95
follow-ups, 212–213
leverage and, 88–89
list of contacts, 91–92, 94
method for contacts, 92
niche markets in, 90–91, 94
outline of, 93–96
presentation in, 92, 95
review and revision of, 96
sample sales plan, 90, 94
time and, 87–88
writing, plan in, 89, 94
Sales presentations. *See* Presentations
Sales tools, 289–299
fast response, 295–296
for future, 296–299
open mind as, 294–295
public speaking as, 292
time management as, 289–291
volunteer work, 291–292

Scripting cold calls, 32–33
Self-esteem, 116, 166–168
Seminars, 285–286
Services. *See also* Delivery
    completed work, 204–205
    products and, 281–282
Sex of customers, 17
Shop talk, 296
Skill learning, 69
Slide presentations, 130
Smiling, 147
Solutions. *See* Problems
    and solutions
Spec project proposals, 215–216,
    228–231
Spin-offs of products, 284–285
Stage fright, 60–61
Steps
    in prospecting process, 28–30
    in sales process, 7–12
Store presentations, 138–139
Style of presentation, 180–182
Subconscious selling, 67, 68
Suggestive selling, 73
Supplies related to products, 281
Support services for products, 281

**T**

Tai Chi, 240
Tailoring product presentations, 21
Talking shop, 296
Target markets, 14–20
    in sales plan, 91–92, 94
Telephone calls. *See also* Cold calls
    cellular phones, 297
    long-distance selling by, 60–61
    meet and greet via, 143
    proposal follow-up, 227

prospecting on telephone, 31–33
    scripting cold calls, 32–33
Television, 100
    home shopping channels, 139
Ten prospects for success, 18–19
Testimonials on products, 139
Thank yous, 218–219
Time
    incentives, 251–252
    negotiation and, 259–260
    past customers, contact of, 219–220
    problems related to, 160–162
    sales plan and, 87–88
    sales tool, time management as,
        289–291
    in trial close, 188–189
Time-frame questions, 157
Tone of voice, 148–150
Training
    disassociation techniques, 73–75
    real-life practice, 71
    rehearsals in, 76–77
    as service, 285–286
Trial close, 9, 11, 185–190
    conditional closing, 187–188
    simple trial close, 187–188
    time and, 188–189

**V**

Value, agreement on, 193–194
Verbal contracts on closing,
    195–196
Verbal cues, 274
Videotapes, information packages
    on, 285
Visual impressions, 72
    anchors in, 275
    in meet and greet, 146–147

portfolios and, 133
as representational system, 272–273
Voice mail, direct mail including
number for, 39
Voice tone, 148–150
Volunteer work, 291–292

## W

Web sites. *See* Internet
Workplace, features-benefits
comparison and, 23
Writing
change-of-life proposals, 231–232
closing in, 195–196

deals in, 179
sales plan in, 89, 94

## Y

Yoga, 240

## Z

Zen Buddhism, 169, 241
ZIP code, mailing lists organized by, 29